Alone With God

Alone with God
Fitting for Service

By

Matilda Erickson Andross

"This sacred shade and solitude, what is it?
'Tis the felt presence of the Deity.
Few are the faults we flatter when alone."

"There is no better fitting for service than
secret communion with the Divine."

1917

PACIFIC PRESS PUBLISHING ASSOCIATION
MOUNTAIN VIEW, CALIFORNIA

Kansas City, Missouri   Portland, Oregon   Brookfield, Illinois
Calgary, Alberta, Canada   Cristobal, Canal Zone

Introduction

A THOUSAND rivulets, in the sudden abundant breaking of a summer shower, flow into a land depression and form oftentimes a beautiful little lake; but in a few days, the hot sun dries the little streams, the lake becomes a pond, and the pond is soon a stagnant pool.

There are many springs, in the vernal season, in the Appalachian ranges; but few remain till the noontide heat of the later summer.

Yet we see the noble river flowing through the drought-stricken land during all the long, torrid days of the burning summer season. It finds its source in the eternal snows and never failing springs of the far-away mountains.

Men die with spent water bottles, journeying over the hot sands of the desert; but the palm tree grows and flourishes. Its roots take hold of the unseen fountains.

Sociability is good, but there may be too much of it. The instinct of gregariousness oftentimes leads us away from the solitude that is needed. Solitude is woven into every character truly strong. Not solitude with one's self alone. That may be in part profitable, but solely it is a source of weakness. All that it may yield us is no better, stronger, higher than ourselves.

Let the solitary moments be with God; for "God to man doth talk in solitude." Converse with Him connects us with the great fountain of life and power, a

Introduction

source-supply inexhaustible, and makes the soul a
spring of crystal sweetness, "whose waters fail not."

It is for the purpose of helping all Christians, but
especially the young, where her heart burden has been
for years, to make the infinite, loving God and Saviour
their source-supply, that this little book is written by
the author. May God bless its mission.

PUBLISHERS.

ALONE WITH GOD

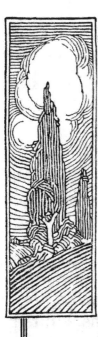

Alone with God

"Alone with God!" The keynote this
    Of every holy life,
The secret power of fragrant growth,
    And victory over strife.

"Alone with God!" In private prayer
    And quietness, we feel
That He draws near our waiting souls,
    And does Himself reveal.

"Alone with God!" Earth's laurels fade;
    Ambition tempts not there;
The world and self are judged just right,
    And no false colors wear.

"Alone with God!" True knowledge gained,
    While sitting at His feet.
We learn life's greatest lessons there,
    Which make for service meet.
                    — *Selected.*

The Supreme Privilege

"Come now, and let us reason together." Isa. 1:18.

"Sweet is the precious gift of prayer,
  To bow before the throne of grace;
To leave our every burden there,
  And gain new strength to run the race;
To gird our heavenly armor on,
  Depending on the Lord alone."

CHAPTER I

SUPPOSE you lived in Washington, D. C., and the president of the United States repeatedly sent you urgent invitations to come to talk over with him privately your personal problems. Would you refuse to go? Suppose he should tell you, over and over again, that he was deeply interested in you; that he understood your perplexities, and was willing to make any sacrifice to help you; that he had already deposited in Riggs's National Bank, *for you,* money enough to obtain the preparation needed for your life work; and that if you would come, he would gladly lay aside all other business, and give you his undivided attention. Would you spurn the offer?

But have you not spurned a better offer? "Come now, and let us reason together," is the invitation the Creator of the universe sends to *you*. Do you heed His call? When He who made the worlds, who keeps the planets moving on schedule time in their appointed orbits, who gives life to each spire of grass, who feeds the sparrows, who supplies all man's necessities, and above all, who "commendeth His love toward us, in that, while we were yet sinners, Christ died for us,"— when He calls you to have a personal interview with Him, do you go?

Do you not often, by your actions, say, "O Lord, I am too busy; I haven't time to talk with You to-day"? Have you not often spurned His invitation to meet Him alone, and then, in your foolish hurry, rushed headlong on to certain defeat in the conflicts of the day? How few there are who consider it absolutely necessary to get their daily program from God! Yet,—

> "If chosen men could never be alone,
> In deep mid-silence open-doored to God,
> No greatness ever had been dreamed or done."

We emphasize service. We repeat the great commission, "Go ye into all the world." We recall how Jesus "lived to bless others," and that He said, "I am among you as he that serveth." We realize that we must copy this aspect of His life, and obey His great command to serve our fellow men wherever we are. So we press on, while whispering to our hungry hearts, "There is no religion without service."

And this is true, so it is right that we should make much of service. But we must not forget that Jesus often sought the solitudes; often He went into the seclusion of the mountains to pray and meditate. Mark tells of His rising a great while before day, to retreat to a quiet place for prayer. "These hours of aloneness were a necessity to Jesus. They were the supreme hours of His life. They were the hours that made His work divine. Out of these hours of retirement He issued to do many things for which they had strengthened and prepared Him." Our strength for service comes from the same source, and we must obtain it in the same way. Unless we have a quiet time when God can speak to us, and when He can pour new strength into our lives, our work will soon become powerless for good, however busily we may serve.

The following incident, related by Mr. McConkey, helps one to appreciate the importance of spending some time alone with God:

"On the shores of Lake Huron, one day last summer, a little group of us were standing on the dock waiting for the arrival of the steamer. All about us was a babel of voices. Presently the young clerk said, 'Come into the fish house.' (It was a fishing village, and there was a little warehouse where the men packed their fish.) We went in with him, and he shut the door, and said, 'Listen.' As we stood there, we could plainly hear the sound of the approaching boat, the peculiar intermittent beating of the paddles of a side-wheel steamer. Then we walked out of the door to the wharf, where the people were talking; and the sound of the approaching steamer vanished. Again with a friend we went into the room, and again we heard the sound clearly and plainly. We were in the place of stillness. There were no voices about to distract, or disturb, or break the silence, and there we could distinctly hear the approaching steamer. We went out and sat down upon the wharf; and in a few minutes, the smoke from the funnels arose above the island. 'What a lesson!' we thought. When we get alone in the chamber of communion with God, we can hear the voice of God; God can reveal His mind to us as nowhere else."

Daniel, when prime minister of Babylon, found it possible to meet God alone three times each day. All that the men asked of Daniel was that he stop praying for thirty days—just thirty days. Many Christians have stopped praying much longer than that, when the only lions in the way were carelessness and spiritual laziness. But with Daniel it was different. He *knew* his God. He had met Him alone often. He regarded that appointment with God as the supreme privilege of life—nay, more, an absolute necessity. And he chose rather to be cast into the lions' den with God, than to live in the palace without Him.

Being alone with God in prayer was the secret of Daniel's strength, of Daniel's wisdom, of Daniel's protection. It always has been the secret of genuine power. Men of power in all ages have been men of prayer; they have been men who insisted on meeting God alone—men who knew that being alone with God was their supreme privilege and their only source of strength. Just think what we might learn in one month in heaven with God. But it is here we must study at His feet to get ready for heaven; and He does not limit our associations with Him. We must decide how much time we will spend with Him, and the relation that shall obtain in these associations. The relation that exists determines the results. It is only when we bring to the Master a fully surrendered will that He can imbue us with unlimited power for service.

Never forget that being alone with God is *your* supreme privilege. You may meet Him alone in the chamber of secret prayer, in your daily work, in the crowded street. Cortland Myers says: "We can come into His presence, we can realize His presence, we can listen and talk and love just as certainly as with an earthly father. This is so wonderful, but so real. It is the best of life." And lest we should omit this best part of life, our Saviour's command to each one of us is: "Enter into thy closet, and when thou hast shut thy door, pray to thy Father which is in secret; and thy Father which seeth in secret shall reward thee openly." The poet passes the command on to us in these words:

"Sometime, between the dawn and dark,
    Go thou, O friend, apart,
That a cool drop of heaven's dew
    May fall into thy heart.
Thus with a spirit soothed and cured
    Of restlessness and pain,
Thou mayest, nerved with force divine,
    Take up thy work again."

You may regret spending too much time with men, but you will never regret spending too much time with God. Then insist on having some time alone with Him each day. Meet Him in the chamber of secret prayer. Spread before Him your life. Do not try to hide any part of it from His all-seeing eye. Close the door of your heart to every disturbing influence, and insist on being alone with your Maker until you have seen Him, and can go forth into life's conflict clothed in His righteousness, and armed with His power.

Still, still with Thee — when purple morning breaketh,
  When the bird waketh, and the shadows flee;
Fairer than the morning, lovelier than the daylight,
  Dawns the sweet consciousness, I am with Thee.

Alone with Thee — amid the mystic shadows,
  The solemn hush of nature newly born;
Alone with Thee in breathless adoration,
  In the calm dew and freshness of the morn.

When sinks the soul, subdued by toil, to slumber,
  Its closing eye looks up to Thee in prayer.
Sweet the repose beneath Thy wings o'ershading,
  But sweeter still to wake and find Thee there!

So shall it be at last, in that bright morning
  When the soul waketh, and life's shadows flee.
Oh, in that hour, fairer than daylight dawning,
  Shall rise the glorious thought, I am with Thee!

              — *Harriet Beecher Stowe.*

Fitted for Service

OH, turn me, mold me, mellow me for use,
　Pervade my being with Thy vital force,
That this else inexpressive life of mine
May become eloquent and full of power,
Impregnated with life and strength divine.
Put the bright torch of heaven into my hand,
That I may carry it aloft,
And win the eye of weary wanderers here below,
To guide their feet into the paths of peace.

I cannot raise the dead,
Nor from the soil pluck precious dust,
Nor bid the sleeper wake,
Nor still the storm, nor bend the lightning back,
Nor muffle up the thunder,
Nor bid the chains fall from off creation's long
　　enfettered limbs;
But I can live a life that tells on other lives,
And makes the world less full of anguish and of
　　pain —
A life that, like the pebble dropped upon the sea,
Sends its wide circles to a hundred shores.

May such a life be mine!
Creator of true life, Thyself the life Thou givest,
Give Thyself that Thou mayest dwell in me, and
　　I in Thee.

　　　　　　　　　　　　— Horatius Bonar.

The Life That Counts

"Be ye therefore perfect." Matt. 5: 48.

"There is only one life that wins, and that is the life of Jesus Christ. Every man may have that life; every man may live that life."— Charles G. Trumbull.

CHAPTER II

"MR. EMERSON is a member of your church, is he not?" I looked in utter surprise at the friend who spoke. "Why, yes," I replied; "I thought you knew he was." "I knew he had been; but I have seen him several times coming from down town Saturdays with a paper sack or a parcel in his hand, and," she continued, "Mildred goes to moving picture shows right along."

The young woman who spoke, although not an Adventist, was quite well acquainted with our church. She was not given to gossiping nor faultfinding; but such flagrant inconsistencies made her wonder whether these comparatively new friends in her circle were church members.

The cloud that settled on my brow, and the few remarks that followed on the subject, could not reveal to her the acuteness of the pain nor the bitterness of the disappointment which her information gave me. I was well acquainted with Mildred Emerson and her father, though in recent years our paths had seldom crossed. I had looked upon him as an ideal Sabbath school superintendent. She, too, was a church member, and blessed with splendid talents for the Master's service. They were lovely people, and I enjoyed their friendship; but why were they drifting? Why were they living lives that contradicted so loudly their profession?

One day, a minister asked a business man if he were a Christian. "No; I cannot say that I am. Still I do not know but I am as good as most church members. For instance, yesterday I got on board the train to ride into Chicago. There came into the coach and sat beside me a woman whom I knew very well, and who is prominent in church work. She claims to be a Christian, and knows that I am not a Christian; but in all that three-hour ride, she did not do another blessed thing but gossip and tell tales about her friends and neighbors, until, when the train stopped in the city, I was heartily glad to get away from her. Now why did that woman who professes to be a follower of Christ, spend all her time in gossip, and have nothing to say about her Master?"

Yes, why do Christians say so little about their Master? And why do their lives so often deny Him? It is a sad fact that thousands of young Christians are content to live on a low plane, showing no desire to grow up into the full stature of Christ Jesus, and having no ambition to live the life that counts. They make no decided effort to overcome besetting sins. They do not lend a helping hand to those in need. In the home, they are not always helpful, but are often unkind. Among their associates, they wield no positive influence. They indulge in the same pleasures, the same reading, and the same vanities as before they became Christians. They do not have enough religion to make them happy in prayer meeting and Christian service, but a little too much for them to be comfortable when indulging in pleasures generally discountenanced. "Oh, what's the harm?" they ask. But such a question is itself a danger signal. It always indicates low spirituality.

It would be well if every young Christian would apply to all things the test John Wesley received from his mother, to guide him in his pleasures during his college life. This is what she wrote him: "Would you judge in the lawfulness or unlawfulness of pleasure, take this rule: Whatever weakens your reason, impairs the tenderness of your conscience, obscures your sense of God, or takes off the relish of spiritual things; whatever increases the authority of your body over your mind,— *that, to you, is sin.*"

There are some young Christians who apparently do nothing,—nothing you can positively condemn, nothing which merits commendation. They are like a savings bank in Maine that was closed by order of the state examiner. Caleb Cobweb says of it: "The institution was entirely sound. There was no lack of confidence in its officers. The bank had been paying dividends regularly. Why, then, was it closed?— Because it had not been growing. It had merely been standing still."

The bank failed, and so will every Christian who is content to live on a low plane. It is very dangerous to be satisfied to stand still, to be content merely to do nothing wrong.

There is said to have been in Sicily, some years ago, a stream that came out of the sulphur beds, and that would turn to sulphur any creature over which it flowed. A small living fish put into a rock basin into which the stream fell, soon lost its power of motion, then its life; and later its very body turned to sulphur. Sin is like that stream. To stand still in one's Christian experience means to become petrified in sin.

And what is more, not only do such Christians lose out themselves, but others stumble over their failures; for, as has been said, every Christian is somebody's Bible. They are stones in the highway of life, over which untrained feet stumble. Their lives are constantly crying out, "The gospel is the power of God unto salvation, but it has not done much for me."

Dr. L. W. Munhall, when a young man, had an experience that should be a warning to all. It occurred before he entered the ministry. With a visiting friend, he went, one evening, to the theater. The next day, he met another friend about whom he was anxious, and once again he asked him to become a Christian. "I never want you to speak to me on that subject again," said the young man. "I saw you last night in the theater; and I have little confidence in a man who professes to be a Christian, but is found in a questionable place of amusement." "I never won him," said Mr. Munhall. "He drifted away from the church and from Christ; and I met him later in the West, a hopeless wreck."

Then why are so many Christians content to live on a low plane?—It is because they are unwilling to pay the price of the life that counts, unwilling to study the Guidebook and follow it closely. I am reminded of a New York firm of which I read some time ago. A business man in South America had ordered a lot of goods from this firm. He gave explicit directions as to how they must be packed. But the employees of that New York firm knew how to pack. They did not require any instructions from South America. So the goods were sent packed in the New York style. Some weeks later, the firm received a letter advising that because they had failed to pack as directed, all the shipment had been destroyed, and they must bear the loss. It seems the goods had to be sent many miles over almost impassable mountains, on the backs of mules. These mules sometimes lost their footing and rolled down the mountain. The goods had to be packed for this contingency. This the New York firm had neglected to do.

Like the New York firm, many young Christians think their own judgment sufficient. However, there is absolute necessity that they follow the directions of the Guide-book; for it explains what the life that counts is, and how one may live it. And often the Christian must read the Book upon his knees. But there is not much Bible study, neither is there much earnest prayer, in the life of the low-plane Christian. Real prayer and real failure in Christian living cannot dwell together. The terms are antagonistic. "The great men of prayer," says Cortland Myers, "have always been known by their pure and loving hearts." Robert F. Horton says: "When a soul is much with God, sin becomes exceedingly sinful, and a great desire is kindled to overcome it. Temptations lose their power. The mask is torn off the face of the tempter, who no longer appears as an angel of light. The secret springs of strength give victory in the struggle with passion and appetite."

The only life that counts is the supremely unselfish life of Jesus Christ. The Bible explains how one may live it, and nature is everywhere trying to teach man that living the life that counts means casting one's self into the furrow of the world's great need. "No bird that cleaves the air, no animal that moves upon the ground, but ministers to some other life. There is no leaf of the forest, or lowly blade of grass, but has its ministry. . . . The flowers breathe fragrance and unfold their beauty in blessing to the world. The sun sheds its light to gladden a thousand worlds. The ocean, itself the source of all our springs and fountains, receives the streams from every land, but takes to give. The mists ascending from its bosom fall in showers to water the earth, that it may bring forth and bud."—*"Desire of Ages," pages 20, 21.*

Yes, nature is a good teacher in the life that counts; and some day, when you are tired of books, and work, and things in general, go and sit down on the grassy bank of a river, and let it tell you the story of life. There is something so human and companionable about a river! As Henry van Dyke says: "It has a life, a character, a voice of its own. . . . It can talk in various tones, loud and low, and on many subjects, grave and gay. . . . For real company and friendship, there is nothing outside of the animal kingdom, that is comparable to a river."

Over the hills and far away is a never failing spring. From it, a small stream runs laughing down the valley—a stream so small that you can step across it. As it goes on and on down the valley, slipping past a hundred hills, darting through fertile fields, skirting thriving cities, it grows until it becomes the irresistible river flowing at your feet. All along the way, the river takes into its bosom water from smaller streams, but it takes to give. All along the way, it is giving *itself.* It waters the grass and the flowers on its banks; the trees slip down their roots and drink its moisture; the birds bathe in its pools; the cattle quench their thirst in its cooling current; the fishes depend on it for food; then as it grows still larger and stronger, it carries the huge vessels of commerce upon its bosom; and finally, *without seeking reward,* its waters slip quietly on, and lose themselves in the eternal deep. This is the story the river tells. It is the story of the unselfish and efficient life—the life that counts.

Does it pay the river to scatter blessings all along its course? Does it pay the rose to fling its sweetness to the world? Does it pay the wheat to grow and feed the hungry millions? Then, too, it pays the Christian to live the life that counts. And every young man and woman may live it; but that life is not to be found on the bargain counter. To live it means to get rid of sin; and "sin is the great-

est power in the universe *except* God." But
as surely as the telescope can find a star in
the heavens, so surely can a soul find its God.
Do you remember the story of the ship's crew
that were half famished for water? Again
and again they signaled to a ship near, "Oh,
give us water!" Each time, the ship signaled
back, "Dip down where you are." This
seemed cruel mockery; but finally, in sheer
despair, they dipped down, and to their as-
tonishment, found that the water was fresh.
They were in the mouth of the Amazon River,
and knew it not.

So you may "dip down" where you are, for
strength to live the life that counts. Keeping
in touch with God is the secret of this life, and
"prayer is the unseen wire stretched from the
very heart of God to the heart of man. It is
just as real and certain as electricity and
gravitation; it is no more mysterious; it is no
less practical. It is just as reasonable to expect to accomplish something by this means as
by any other law or invention." Yes, prayer
is the great reality in life. "I prayed God to
make me an extraordinary Christian," wrote
the great and good Whitefield, in his diary;
and his life was an evidence that his prayer
was heard and answered. Edwards says of

him, "In spirit, in prayerfulness, in ceaseless labor, in love to Christ, and in earnest and tireless efforts to win men from their sins to Him, he was, as he had prayed to be, 'an extraordinary Christian.' "

To be an extraordinary Christian, to live the life that counts, means supreme happiness. Dr. W. T. Grenfell says of the beginning of his career in the life that counts: "In my own life, when, at the feet of D. L. Moody, I first accepted Christ as my Master, my Sundays, my only free days, formerly devoted to the usual young men's amusements and occupations, I devoted to holding open-air services and to visiting underground lodging houses in Ratcliffe Highway. The change was so sudden that I was able to appreciate the contrast in my sensations; for it was a tremendous effort to me to be preaching at all, and that more especially in the open air and in the neighborhoods frequented by my fellow students. I had enjoyed the sensations of athletic victories, and I had carried off more than one material trophy; but there has never been any question in my mind as to which was the truest joy, that afforded by self-serving, or that by Christ-serving, either as first I saw it

then, or as, after twenty-five years, with some-
what altered perspective, I see it now."

Secret prayer is the breath of the life that
counts; for "God fades out of the life of those
who do not pray." And with secret prayer
goes personal Bible study. These two absolutely necessary things may be reinforced in
various ways. Be ambitious to succeed in
whatever you undertake. "Let not dead yesterday unborn to-morrow shame," but work in
the spirit of the artist who, when asked which
of his pictures he considered the best, replied,
"My next one." Let not yesterday's mistakes
crush you. Talk them over with God, and
then remember that *to-day* is a new beginning.
Make the most of it. Work helps to preserve
purity, and is one secret of increased strength.
Have faith in your work. Believe that it
merits your best efforts, and then throw yourself into it.

Men and women of wide experience tell us
that carefulness in diet, regularity in bathing,
and faithfulness in exercise, are good helpers
in the struggle for pure lives. Good reading
is another. Charles Dickens said that his love
for good books was one of his strongest de-
fenses against temptation. Many young
people have been kept from wrong through

their devotion to hobbies. Ion Keith Falconer had a good hobby. Every week, he devoted one evening to gospel work among the poor in London. Charles Kingsley, when asked the secret of his beautiful life, replied, "I had a friend." Then gather around you good, faithful friends, by *being* such a friend to others; and above all, make God your friend, for "He passeth all the rest." But always remember that "except the Lord keep the city, the watchman waketh but in vain." Good resolutions cannot withstand the daily temptations. Unreserved consecration to God is the only sure safeguard. Then surrender all to Him, and trust Him; for He is "able to keep you from falling." As another says, "Trust God, respect yourself, be strong *in the strength of Christ,* and you may yet tread upon the young lion and the adder."

The world is languishing for want of young men and women who will live the life that counts. Will you? God wishes to write in your heart His law of love and purity. He wants your life to be in this sinful world what the pure lily is in the stagnant pool. More than that, He wants you to help others to regain their lost heritage; He wants you to help other young Christians to live the life that counts. Does not your heart ache when you see young women selling a useful, noble career for some fleeting pleasure? Are you not pained to see young men with bright prospects go galloping on to ruin? Then step into the breach! Be a Daniel! Be an Esther! When millions are perishing, we have no time to think of ease or selfish gratification. For your own sake, for the sake of others, and for Christ's sake, live the life that counts. Follow Paul's advice to Timothy, "Keep thyself pure," for purity is power. Do right, and remember that God not only forgives the past, but provides strength for the present, and hope for the future.

Do not say: "I have made too many mistakes. It's no use." One day, Michelangelo was looking over some ruins. Among them was a piece of marble that had been thrown away as useless. But the artist's eye saw something of great value in that piece of discarded marble; and he carved from it an exquisitely beautiful statue. So the great Architect of souls sees wonderful possibilities in your life; and He wants to make of it a life that will be a blessing to the world—a better life than you even have dared to dream of, for "higher than the highest human thought can ever reach is God's ideal for His children."

The saddest sight on earth is not that of a young Christian laid away to rest beneath the turf just at the moment when others enter their life work; the greatest of all tragedies is the tragedy of the young person who fails to live the life that counts.

Could we for but one brief moment shut ourselves away from the busy, bustling world, and get a true picture of life and all that concerns us, we would be persuaded that, cost what it may, the life that counts is worth while; for to live it, means to be true to God, and true to our fellow men; it means an irresistible power for doing good, and an unfailing happiness, which the world can neither give nor take away. You may live this life; will you?

———

"Oh, do not pray for easy lives; pray to be stronger men. Do not pray for tasks equal to your powers; pray for powers equal to your tasks. Then the doing of your work shall be no miracle, but you shall be a miracle. Every day, you shall wonder at yourself, at the richness of life which has come to you by the grace of God."—*Phillips Brooks.*

STIR ME!

Stir me, oh, stir me, Lord! I care not how;
  But stir my heart in passion for the world.
Stir me to give, to go — but most to pray.
  Stir till Thy blood-red banner be unfurled
O'er lands that still in heathen darkness lie —
O'er deserts where no cross is lifted high.

Stir me, oh, stir me, Lord, till all my heart
  Is filled with strong compassion for these souls;
Till Thy compelling "must" drive me to prayer;
  Till Thy constraining love reach to the poles,
Far north and south, in burning, deep desire;
Till east and west are caught in love's great fire!

Stir me, oh, stir me, Lord, till prayer is pain,
  Till prayer is joy — till prayer turns into praise!
Stir me till heart and mind and will — yea, all —
  Is wholly Thine, to use through all the days.
Stir till I learn to pray "exceedingly."
Stir till I learn to wait expectantly.

Stir me, oh, stir me, Lord! Thy heart was stirred
  By love's intensest fire, till Thou didst give
Thine only Son, Thy best beloved One,
  E'en to the dreadful cross, that I might live;
Stir me to give myself so back to Thee,
That Thou canst give *Thyself* again through me.

Stir me, oh, stir me, Lord! For I can see
  Thy glorious triumph day begin to break.
The dawn already gilds the eastern sky.
  Oh, church of Christ, arise! Awake! Awake!
Oh, stir us, Lord, as heralds of that day!
The night is past — our King is on His way!
                        — *Bessie Porter Head.*

(30)

Equipment for Service

"The effectual fervent prayer of a right-
eous man availeth much." James 5: 16.

"God's greatest agency for winning men back to
Himself is the prayers of other men."— C. Myers, in
"Real Prayer."

CHAPTER III

A GREAT minister in London had a church that was very rich. The social standing was high, and the best society was in it. He was an orator, a literary genius, a poet; he wrote books. But regardless of all his rare ability, the pews of that church became less and less occupied. At last, he went on his knees before God, and asked the reason. He wanted a change in his life; he felt he must have power; he pleaded with God to show him what was the great necessity; and he tells us that there, while on his knees, alone with God, he heard a voice as distinct as any human voice say, "Live the life, live the life." The minister decided to live the life that counts, and the result was that the religious conditions in that part of London were transformed.

Once when Evangelist Wilbur Chapman was in England, he asked the late General Booth what he considered the secret of his remarkable success in Christian service. The great soul winner was silent for a moment. A tear trickled down his cheek as he said: "If there is any secret in my success as a soul winner, it is this: Since I first caught a glimpse of the poor in London, God has had all there is of me."

At the Student Volunteer Convention held in Rochester, New York, in 1910, Sherwood Eddy said: "I remember fifteen years ago, before going to India, sitting down one night with my roommate, who is now in China, and saying to him: 'What are we going to tell them out on the field? What message have we for men? Are we merely going out to tell them *about* Christ? If so, it would be cheaper to send out Bibles and tracts. Can we tell them we *know* that Jesus Christ saves and satisfies, and that He keeps us more than conquerors day by day? I am not satisfied. I do not feel that I have a message such as I need for men out there, nor the experience, nor the power. If we have not, is not that *the one thing* we need before we leave this country—to know Him?'"

So these Christian workers, like all others who have been successful soul winners, testify that he who would be pre-eminently successful must live the life that counts. Wilbur Chapman puts it this way: "God will never use you as a great soul winner until He has all there is of you—never."

It is when the channel of life is open, cleared of sin, that God can stretch His mighty arm through it to save others. Think how the Panama Canal has transformed the commerce of the world. The oceans have not changed. Through the centuries, they have been waiting to fill that canal; but only when all obstacles were removed, could they press in to fill it, and make it a waterway of the nations, a blessing to the world.

Just as Bishop Hannington said, "I have purchased the way to Uganda with my life," so living *the life* is the price of success in Christian service. A man said one day, "I wish I could be a Henry Martyn." His friend shouted back, "Then live Henry Martyn's life." If you would be a successful soul winner, live the life of a successful soul winner. That is all.

And to be a soul winner is life's greatest opportunity. Mrs. Taylor, after years of

3—Alone

hard work in China, said, "Life holds no privilege more precious than that of giving itself for the salvation of the lost." Often I think of the words of Ellen Stone. At the Student Volunteer Convention held in Nashville in 1906, she told us about her release from the bandits who had taken her captive. The story of her experience had made me shudder; so I was much astonished to hear her say, almost in tears, "Oh, I want to go back to Albania!" About four years later, I saw her again. Circumstances were still holding her in this country, but there was traced on her beaming face the same longing to return to the land of her captivity.

When Florence Nightingale heard the call to definite service, she chose to forsake the so-called luxuries of life, and give her time to the sufferers of the Crimean War. A young man heard the same call; and when asked why he was going to Japan as a missionary, he replied, "Because I feel it is the best investment I can make of my life." And truly it is.

Angels would gladly do the work that young men and women of the twentieth century have before them; but God has commissioned Christians to be colaborers with Him in the great work of saving a lost world.

Angels stand ready to help each worker. They are "ministering spirits, sent forth to minister for them who shall be heirs of salvation."

For several thousand years, the work of saving a lost world has been heaven's most important business. So much in earnest is God that He gave His only Son to come to this world, to live and die for its accomplishment; and all through the centuries, He has kept large armies of angels to help men and women in this all-important work. Surely the chief business of Christians, as Christ's representatives, is to save souls. Amos R. Wells has said, "The Christian that is not making other Christians is as much a contradiction in terms as a fire that is not heating, or a flame that gives no light." Charles G. Finney once said: "The great object for which Christians are converted and live in this world is to pull sinners out of the fire. If they do not effect this, they had better be dead."

But what is the relation of prayer to Christian service? Look back over the history of Christian service, and you will find that the men and women who have lifted the world spiritually, have saturated their lives with prayer. It is recorded of Luther, whose name

stands for the great Reformation of the six-
teenth century, that when especially busy, he
would say that he must spend more time than
usual in prayer, in order to accomplish most.

The biographer of David Brainerd writes
of him: "He was, as all Christ's true men and
women must be, mighty in prayer. It was his
habit to spend long nights in the dark forests,
with strong cryings to God, a very wrestling
with the Almighty for the salvation of sinners.
His whole life seems to have been divided between preaching and prayer, hastening to the
woods, after some discouragement, to meet
his Lord for renewal of faith and confidence,
or, with a whole heart of thanksgiving, casting
himself on the ground, and crying, 'Not unto
us, O Lord, not unto us, but unto Thy name
give glory.'"

Columba, Livingstone, and Whitefield died
upon their knees. D. L. Moody says, "Bax-
ter stained the study walls with praying
breath, and after he was anointed with the
unction of the Holy Ghost, sent a river of living water over Kidderminster, and converted
hundreds." John Knox prayed, "O God,
give me Scotland or I die;" and such a power
was he in his work, that the Catholic Mary on
her throne would say, "I fear John Knox

more than an army of twenty thousand men."
R. F. Horton, in his book "Victory in Christ,"
says: "I think all the victors who have overcome, whose bright names star the heavens and
will shine forever and ever, made and kept
their hours of prayer. If these souls had not
insisted on being alone in the deep mid-silence
between themselves and God, their great deeds
might never have been attempted, but it is
sure they could never have been done." The
greatest of all missionaries, who at thirty-three
years of age could say, "I have finished the
work Thou gavest Me to do," prayed, prayed
much, prayed as never man prayed.

These are a few of the great host of Christian workers who join with Neesima, the
Christian educator of Japan, in saying that
"we must advance upon our knees" if we
would succeed. "Our victory, therefore, over
self and sin, or other souls, or over difficulties
and impossibilities," says another, "depends
on the free and unhindered union with God by
which we become willing instruments in His
hands. And that union is the result of con-
tinuous prayer."

To the praying Christian, the *chief business
of life is to save souls;* and it should be. God
has not made the salvation of this lost world

a secondary business; neither should we. As
Forrest Hallenbeck says, "There is only one
passion for the blood-bought heart; that is the
all-controlling purpose which brought the Son
of God from the skies, and drove Him to the
cross—the passion for the salvation of men."
This was the passion of Vassar's heart. A but-
terfly of fashion to whom he spoke in a hotel
realized it. When her husband came home,
and she told him of the strange man who
had asked her whether she were a Christian,
he said, "Why did you not tell him it was none
of his business?" but she replied, "O husband,
if you had seen the expression on his face,
and heard the earnestness with which he spoke,
you would have thought it was his business."

Have you ever stopped to think that if
business men did their work in the slipshod,
half-hearted manner in which some Christians
go into soul winning, they would be bankrupt
inside of three years? Genuine prayer is the
secret of genuine service; but there can be no
earnest prayer for the cause in which one is
only half-heartedly interested. "Suppose
some one were to offer me a thousand dollars
for every soul that I might earnestly try to
lead to Christ. Would I endeavor any more
to lead souls to Him than I do now? Is

it possible that I would attempt to do *for money*, even at the risk of blunders or ridicule, what I shrink from doing now in obedience to God's command? Is my love of money stronger than my love of God or of souls? How feeble, then, my love of God! Perhaps this explains why I am not a soul winner."

A young man on the shores of Lake Michigan heard the distress signal of a sinking boat. Throwing his coat on the sand, he plunged into the snowy billows. Again and again he swam back to the wreck, until he had rescued seventeen persons. Then he dropped, exhausted, on the beach. It was too much. He was seized with a violent fever, and for three weeks he was delirious. Often he would moan: "Oh, did I do my best? Did I do my best?" That boy loved his fellow men, and was willing to "spend and be spent" for them. If all Christian workers manifested the same intensity of loving interest in their efforts to save souls, what wonders would be wrought!

I think it was John Wesley who said, "Give me ten men who hate nothing but sin, who fear nothing but God, and who seek nothing but the salvation of their fellow men, and I will set the world on fire." But how can we learn to love souls as God does?—This intense love

for souls, this zeal in Christian service, will be
yours and mine as soon as God has *all* there is
of us; for somehow *the same prayer that
draws us close to God draws us close to our
fellow men.*

God wants *you* to help Him save your rela-
tives and friends, and all whom He sends to
you. He wants you to keep in close touch
with Him through prayer, that He may keep
you supplied with all the power you need for
service. He is counting on you, counting on
me—counting on our seizing every opportunity around us. Let us remember that some
opportunities come but once, then they are
gone forever. They are like the ship that
came to the Golden Gate one night and signaled for the harbor pilot to come and take
it in. The night was very stormy, and he
did not go. The captain dared not let his ship
remain in the shallow water near treacherous
rocks; and finally, in despair, he turned out
to sea again. Nothing was ever heard of that
ship afterward. The opportunity to save it
was gone forever. And since some of our opportunities come but once, we need to pray
with the young girl who said: "O Lord, fill
me to overflowing! I cannot hold much, but
I can overflow a great deal." So can we; and

when we are constantly overflowing with the love of God for others, we shall not miss the opportunities He sends us.

During a large Sunday school convention held in Chicago, a woman came to one of the Christian workers, and told him about her lost boy in San Francisco. The worker was going to that city; and she asked him to look up her boy, and try to save him. As she turned to go, she handed the worker a slip of paper. He unfolded it, and read: "Won't you go once? Won't you go twice? Won't you go a hundred times? Won't you go *till you get him?*" So, dear young friend, as God calls you to try to save those about you, won't *you* go once? Won't *you* go twice? Won't *you* go a hundred times? Won't *you go till you get them?* Go first into the chamber of secret prayer, to connect with the great dynamo of heaven; and then go forth, in the power of God, to win others to Him.

The sunset burns across the sky;
Upon the air its warning cry.
The curfew tolls from tower to tower.
O children, 'tis the last, last hour!

We hear His footsteps on the way!
Oh, work while it is called to-day,
Constrained by love, endued with power,
O children, in this last, last hour!

— *Clara Thwaites.*

I've Found a Friend

I've found a Friend, oh, such a Friend!
  He loved me ere I knew Him;
He drew me with the cords of love,
  And thus He bound me to Him.
And round my heart still closely twine
  Those ties, which naught can sever;
For I am His, and He is mine,
  Forever and forever.

I've found a Friend, oh, such a Friend!
  He bled, He died, to save me;
And not alone the gift of life,
  But His own self, He gave me.
Naught that I have, my own I call;
  I hold it for the Giver;
My heart, my strength, my life, my all,
  Are His, and His forever.

I've found a Friend, oh, such a Friend!
  All power to Him is given,
To guard me on my upward course,
  And lead me safe to heaven.
The eternal glories gleam afar,
  To nerve my faint endeavor;
So now to watch, to work, to war,
  And thus to rest forever.

I've found a Friend, oh, such a Friend,
  So kind, and true, and tender,
So wise a Counselor and Guide,
  So mighty a Defender!
From Him who loveth me so well,
  What power my soul can sever?
Shall life or death, or earth or hell?
  No; I am His forever.
                    — Selected.

Jesus and I Are Friends

"Ye are My friends, if ye do whatsoever I command you." John 15: 14.

*"Personal contact with Christ, to sit down in com-
panionship with Him,— this is our need."—"Education," page 261.*

CHAPTER IV

*T*HE late J. R. Miller had been lecturing
in Paris. After one of the evening services, a man came to him, and said: "Dr. Miller, I have forgotten almost everything you
said except this one sentence: 'To me, religion means just one thing: Jesus and I are
friends.'" J. R. Miller's life, pressed full of
untiring service, was a beautiful demonstration of the transforming influence of Jesus
upon the lives of those who love Him, of those
who can say, "Jesus and I are friends."

Luther Burbank has made wonderful
changes in fruits and flowers. He has taken
away their objectionable features, and devel-
oped their points of beauty and usefulness.
But far more wonderful is the transformation
wrought by Jesus in the lives of His friends.
Most young people have some thorns in their

(43)

characters; but Jesus promises that His friendship, if accepted, shall free them from every undesirable trait. Phillips Brooks says: "If you will let Him walk with you in your streets, sit with you in your offices, and be with you in your homes, and teach you in your churches, and abide with you as the living presence in your hearts, you too shall know what freedom is; and while you do your duties, be above your duties; and while you own yourselves the sons of men, know you are the sons of God."

The sentence, "Jesus and I are friends," contains the secret of the Christian life; and every Christian has the privilege of finding in Jesus a real personal friend. John R. Mott says: "Now I maintain that it is possible and practicable for each Christian to have Christ become and remain a great reality in his life; to be conscious of His presence; to experience beyond doubt His actual help in breaking the power of temptation, in lifting the burden of sin, in shedding light in times of doubt on questions which perplex us, in affording a sense of companionship in times of sorrow or severe trial; to have Him become a vastly more potent factor in transforming character and energizing life than any other person or persons, living or dead. Christ then becomes not merely One who lived and taught and wrought nearly two thousand years ago; not simply an inspiring memory of beneficent or historical character, for example, like Martin Luther, or William the Silent; not some vague, impersonal influence; but—

" 'A living, bright reality,
  More dear, more intimately nigh,
  Than e'en the sweetest earthly tie.' "

Charles G. Trumbull says of an interview with Dr. John D. Adams: "I learned from him that what he counted his greatest spiritual asset was his unvarying consciousness of the actual presence of Jesus. Nothing bore him up so, he said, as the realization that Jesus was *always* with him in actual presence; and that this was so, independently of his own notions as to how Jesus would manifest His presence. Moreover, he said that Christ was the home of his thoughts. Whenever his mind was free from other matters, it would turn to Christ, and he would talk aloud to Christ when he was alone—on the street, anywhere— as easily as to a human friend, so real to him was Jesus' actual presence."

The world owes much to the friends of Jesus. In all ages, they have lifted up the

Redeemer of the world, that He might draw all to Himself. Their lives have demonstrated His power to save from sin; their faithful service has helped to interpret to the world the love of the sinners' Friend. The world's greatest need to-day is the need of Christians who can say truly, "Jesus and I are friends." Jesus is the highest interpretation of unselfishness; and the more we associate with Him, the more we shall be like Him. Our friendship will result in a life of unselfish service, for "He lived to bless others." As Raphael admired and studied and believed in Michelangelo, and thus partook of his genius, so we may cling to Christ and love and serve Him, and thus become like Him. In time, we shall be able to say, with Paul, "Nevertheless I live; yet not I, but Christ liveth in me;" and that will be living the life that counts.

But he who would enjoy friendship must meet the conditions of friendship. There is no genuine friendship without some sacrifice; for, as Woodrow Wilson, when president of Princeton, said, "The object of love is to serve, not to win." Yet, cost what it may, "friendship," as Edward Everett Hale once said, "is the greatest luxury in life." The friendship of Jesus is more than a luxury; it

is the secret of eternal life; it is the pearl of
great price; and to buy it, *costs all.* Jesus
says, "If any man will come after Me, let him
deny himself, and take up his cross, and follow
Me;" and again, "Ye are My friends, if ye
do whatsoever I command you." In another
place, He says, "Blessed are the pure in heart:
for they shall see God."

Victory over sin, through consecration, is
needed in order to be close friends with Jesus.
Abraham was known as "the friend of God,"
and he was willing to lay life's dearest treas-
ure upon the altar at his Friend's command.
The psalmist asks, "Who shall ascend into the
hill of the Lord?" and then answers, "He that
hath clean hands, and a pure heart." When
George Müller decided to enter the circle of
Jesus' friends, he was compelled to give up
some dissipated young chums who refused to
join him. He paid the price, as have thousands of others, and became a great blessing
to those about him; for truly, only he who has
Jesus for his personal friend can be a genuine
friend to others.

One time, St. Augustine caught himself
praying, "O Lord, give me purity, but not
yet." And so, some Christians are saying,
"Lord, give me unselfishness, but let me have

my own way in this thing;" or, "Lord, give
me humility, but do not require me to come
down from the position I have already taken
before others;" or, "Lord, give me purity, but
let a certain picture still hang in the chambers
of my imagery." "If we have a thousand
things, and give up nine hundred and ninety-
nine to Christ, but still hold on to one, Christ
will not be real to us. He is the Lord of *all,*
or not Lord at all. He requires everything
of us; and not until we make a complete surrender does He fully disclose Himself to us.
The more we identify ourselves with His aims,
desires, and ideals, the nearer and more real
He will seem to us."

Does the friendship of Jesus mean slavery?—No, a hundred times, no. But Jesus
has paid our way to heaven; He is the only
one who has charted the course there; and our
only safety lies in following our Friend and
Guide, in every detail. All realize this in a
way; and in the hours of deepest distress, even
the enemies of Jesus turn to Him for comfort
and help. While a certain infidel writer was
finishing one of his books on atheism, he was
called to the bedside of his little daughter, who
was dying. "Papa," she said, "I am going to
die. Mamma says Jesus will save me. You

say there is no God.   Now what shall I do?"
Tears filled the father's eyes, his shoulders
shook, and in broken words he said, "Darling,
you better accept your mother's Christ, and
be saved."

The friendship of Jesus is worth *everything*
to the young Christian, not alone when he is
brought face to face with death, but to-day,
and every day.   First of all, He sympathizes
with us in all our sorrows, disappointments,
troubles, and temptations; for "He was in all
points tempted like as we are," that He might
"succor them that are tempted."

> "He knows the bitter, weary way,
> The endless striving day by day,
> The souls that weep, the souls that pray —
> He knows.
>
> "He knows how hard the way has been,
> The clouds that come our lives between,
> The wounds the world has never seen —
> He knows."

There are corners in your heart that no
human eye can see; there are trials that no
human friend can help you bear; there are
perplexities and longings which you can never
explain to an earthly friend.   But Jesus
knows, He understands, He loves, and He
wants to help and comfort.   The beautiful
poem about His care, written by Fanny Edna
Stafford, is for *you:*

4—Alone

"Somebody knows when your heart aches,
  And everything seems to go wrong;
Somebody knows when the shadows
  Need chasing away with a song;
Somebody knows when you're lonely,
  Tired, discouraged, and blue;
Somebody wants you to know Him,
  And know that He dearly loves you.

"Somebody cares when you're tempted,
  And the world grows dizzy and dim;
Somebody cares when you're weakest,
  And farthest away from Him;
Somebody grieves when you've fallen,
  Though you are not lost from His sight;
Somebody waits for your coming,
  Taking the gloom from your night.

"Somebody loves you when weary;
  Somebody loves you when strong;
Always is waiting to help you,
  Watches you, one of the throng
Needing His friendship so holy,
  Needing His watch-care so true.
His name? — We call His name Jesus.
His people? — Just I and just *you*."

For the friend of Jesus there is peace, undisturbed peace, in this world of trouble. "In the Pitti Palace at Florence hangs a picture which represents a stormy sea, with wild waves, and black clouds, and fierce lightning flashing across the sky. Wrecks float on the angry waters, and here and there a human face is seen. Out of the midst of the waves a rock rises, against which the waters dash in vain. It towers high above the crest of the waves. In a cleft of the rock are some tufts of grass and green herbage, with sweet flowers blooming; and amid these a dove is seen sitting on her nest, quiet and undisturbed by the wild fury of the storm or the mad dashing of the waves." The picture fitly represents the peace of the Christian amid the sorrows and trials of the world. He is hidden in the cleft of the Rock of Ages, and nestles securely in the bosom of God's unchanging love.

How comfortable and happy you are in the presence of a sympathetic friend whom you trust implicitly! You understand each other's half spoken thoughts, and even periods of silence do not arouse suspicion. But no one has ever tasted the deepest joys of friendship, who has not made Jesus his closest friend; for, as David says, "In Thy presence is fullness of joy; at Thy right hand there are pleasures forevermore." Henry Martyn's diary contained this sentence, which bears out the psalmist's thought: "My chief enjoyment was the enjoyment of God's presence."

When Gladstone was asked, "What is the most important question before England?" he replied, "The most important question before England to-day or any day is one's personal relation to Jesus Christ." That is the most important question before young people to-day. "Remember now thy Creator in the days of thy youth." Young friends, "What think ye of Christ?" Can you say, "Jesus and I are friends"? When an old man, Darwin confessed that he had failed to become personally acquainted with Jesus when young, and somehow in old age, he lost the ability to cultivate the friendship of the best of all friends. One day, a Christian worker sat down and talked with the learned Professor Huxley about the Saviour, His love, His power to save from sin, and to transform the lives of those who come to Him. Professor Huxley's eyes filled with tears as he stretched out his right hand, and said, "Oh, I would give *this* if I only could believe that." Truly youth is the golden age of opportunity; and the greatest opportunity of all is to make Jesus a close personal friend now, for "youth comes twice to none."

How can this friendship be formed? How can young Christians make Jesus Christ a real personal friend? Years ago, there was an old German professor whose beautiful life was a marvel to his students. Some of them resolved to know the secret of it; so one of their number hid in the study where the old professor usually spent his evenings. It was late when the teacher came in. He was very tired, but he sat down and spent an hour with his Bible. Then he bowed his head in secret prayer; and finally closing the Book of books, he said, "Well, Lord Jesus, we're on the same old terms." Just so in the chamber of secret prayer and devotional Bible study, every young Christian may meet Jesus, and learn to know Him as He is—the best of all personal friends.

In a certain chapel, there is a bust of our Lord before which a stool is placed, that the beholder may kneel and look. To the one who is standing up, the bust has no beauty. It is essential to kneel in order to see the glory and beauty of the countenance. So, as long as we stand in self-satisfaction, we see no beauty in Christ; but the moment there is humbling of soul before God on account of sin, we behold an excellence we did not see before in Christ. We should study Him often upon our knees before the open Book.

To *know Him* is life's highest attainment; and at all costs, every Christian should strive to be "on the same old terms" with Him. The reality of Jesus comes as a result of secret prayer, and a personal study of the Bible, that is devotional and sympathetic. Christ becomes real to the person who studies the Bible record of His life, His work, His words. He remains real to the one who continues to study Christ, and meditates upon Him. J. R. Mott says: "Christ becomes real to one who persists in the cultivation of the habit of reminding one's self of His presence." "By associating with those to whom Christ is a great reality, He may be made more real to us. We should associate not only with living Christians who know Christ at first hand, but also those who in other times lived near to Him." He also says that whenever his faith becomes dim, or Christ becomes unreal, all he needs to do is to spend some time with the biographies of persons who have been intimately acquainted with Christ.

Then, too, the Holy Spirit will help the young Christian to know Jesus as a close personal friend. David Hill, a missionary in China, once said, "I have lately felt great nearness to God in pleading for the salvation of souls here." The more we try to help others to know Him, the more real He will become to us; the more we sacrifice for Him, the better we shall know Him, and the more we shall love Him.

"And not for sign in heaven above
Or earth beneath we look,
Who know, with John, His smile of love,
With Peter, His rebuke."

If, after you and Jesus have become friends, He should grow unreal again, remember that it is your fault; for as an editorial in the *Sunday School Times* says: "Nothing ever dims our consciousness of the personal presence and fullness of Christ but our own sin. We may not know what the sin is that is dulling our joy in Him. We may rebel and protest, trying to make ourselves think that it is not our fault, but that He has arbitrarily and unjustly withdrawn His presence from us. That will not set matters right. Nothing but a fresh surrender, in an abandonment of confessed helplessness and worthlessness and utter dependence upon Christ, in faith, will enable Him to surcharge our life with Himself, and make Himself known and felt again in the old joyous overwhelming of our being. The electricity cannot make the carbon filament glow with light and fire until that filament is insulated from everything else, and is yielded up to the electricity alone. Nor can we glow with the light and fire of Christ until we have let Him cut us off from everything else, insulate us into yielded and complete conductors of Himself and the current of His love and power. When the light ceases in the electric lamp, you know there is a break somewhere; either the insulation or the connection is not complete. It may take considerable search to find the break; but you know it is there. So of our interruptions of fellowship with God in Christ. Connection with Him, and disconnection with all else—both of these must be complete, or He cannot do for us what He would."

Nothing, absolutely nothing, can separate us from this Friend, except our own sins. He never forsakes those who cling to Him. Paul says, "I am persuaded, that neither death, nor life, nor angels, nor principalities, nor powers, nor things present, nor things to come, nor height, nor depth, nor any other creature, shall be able to separate us from the love of God, which is in *Christ Jesus our Lord.*"

> "Jesus whispers, 'I am with you
>   In the sunshine, in the cloud,
> When the spirit is exalted,
>   When the stricken head is bowed.'
>
> "Jesus whispers, 'I am with you
>   In the battle every day;
> Standing by you in the conflict,
>   Going with you all the way.'
>
> "Jesus whispers, 'I am with you
>   In the hour of deepest need;

When the way is dark and lonesome,
    I am with you, I will lead.'

"Jesus whispers, 'I am with you —
    With you still, whate'er betide;
In the sunlight or the shadow,
    I am ever at thy side.' "

A little girl lying at the point of death called her father. She put her arms around his neck, and asked, "Father, what shall I tell Jesus is the reason you do not love Him?" The father's heart was broken, and after a moment's silence, he said, "Oh, my child, tell Him that I do love Him." Do you love Him? Can *you* say to-day, "Jesus and I are friends"? Jesus wants *you* to be His friend. He is not trying to keep away from you. Oh, no! He not only says, "Him that cometh to Me I will in no wise cast out," but He is trying to win *every* young person who is not His friend. He is standing patiently at the door of every unentered heart, knocking for admission, and saying, "I have loved you with an everlasting love." What are you telling Him is your reason for not loving Him?

"O Jesus, Thou art standing
    Outside the fast-closed door,
In lowly patience waiting
    To cross the threshold o'er;
We bear the name of Christian,
    His name and sign we bear;
Oh, shame, thrice shame upon us,
    To keep Him standing there!"

The Living Word

COUNTLESS volumes have been written on this theme without exhausting it, and witnesses to the Bible still multiply. The mighty past is speaking. God is bringing forth its testimony. Egypt, Assyria, Babylon, have broken the silence of the ages. The moldering monuments, the buried cities, the sandy deserts, the sculptured rocks, have found a voice. Sinai and Petra, Horeb and Hermon, echo the sacred oracles. Memphis and Tyre, Tadmor and Nineveh, have risen from their graves. The painted papyrus, the pictured walls, the stony tablets, the rusted medals and coins, bring forth their testimony. The ruins, the rivers, the mountains, and the seas cry out, "Thy word is truth." And the living witness, as well as the dead. The Samaritan still lingers at Sychar; the Jew still wanders in every land. The church of Christ still lives, and spreads throughout the world. The gospel still regenerates. The promised Spirit still sanctifies, and witnesses in Christian hearts. In a word, history and experience confirm the Scriptures, and assure us that through the prophets of the Old Testament and the apostles of the New, and above all, through His Son, God Himself has spoken to our race; and that the word which He has spoken liveth and abideth forever.— *H. Grattan Guinness.*

(58)

Alone with God's Word

"Search the Scriptures." John 5: 39.

"The Bible, the whole Bible, nothing but the Bible, is the standard and the rule of Christianity. To know its meaning for ourselves, to rely on its promises, to trust in its Redeemer, to obey Him from delight of love, and to refuse to follow any other teaching, is Christianity itself."— T. W. Medhurst, in "The Fundamentals."

CHAPTER V

A RETURNED missionary was addressing a group of young ministers who were planning to go to China. In his closing remarks, he said: "You may learn to speak Chinese glibly, you may adopt Chinese customs, eat with chopsticks, and even wear a cue; but unless you are *faithful in secret prayer and personal Bible study,* you will be failures as missionaries in China." Secret prayer and personal Bible study go together; they are inseparable. Prayer is the breath of the spiritual life, and personal Bible study is its food.

R. F. Horton, in "Victory in Christ," says: "The one sure and never failing method of living the victorious life is daily study of the

. Bible,—*study,* not hasty reading; *daily,* not at fitful intervals. That study must be *with prayer,* and faith, and a single-eyed desire to know the will of God and to do it. Such a devotional and habitual use of the Bible, beyond all dispute, leads to a full experience of God's love, of Christ's saving power, of the indwelling of the Holy Spirit. The Bible of any one who has lived the life with which we are concerned is yellow with years, thin at the edges with constant turning of the paper, scored with the lines and marks which are all monuments of truths seen and help received, stained with tears which have been often tears of penitence, but sometimes tears of joy, falling like a tender rain when the glory of God has suddenly shone out from the page."

The lives of Christians in all countries and in all ages demonstrate the transforming power of God's word. Some one asked a young man how he knew the Bible is inspired; he replied, "Because it inspires me." Alexander Maclaren attributed his life of power to two things: first, the habit of personal Bible study (it is said that for sixty years his study of the Scriptures in the original was not interrupted for a single day); second, the place he gave Christ in his life.

Wherever the Bible goes, it helps to bring about a feeling of brotherly love. An English trader was reminded of this when he landed on a once cannibal island. Seeing a native studying his Bible, the trader said to him, "Oh, that Book is out of date in our country." "It is?" asked the native. "Well, if it were out of date here, you would have been eaten long ago."

"Years ago, a young infidel was traveling in the West with his uncle, a banker, and they were not a little anxious for their safety when they were forced to stop for a night in a rough wayside cabin. There were two rooms in the house; and when they retired for the night, they agreed that the young man should sit with his pistols, and watch until midnight, and then awaken his uncle, who should watch until morning. Presently they peeped through a crack, and saw their host, a rough looking old man, in his bearskin suit, reach up and take down a Bible; and after reading it a while, he knelt and began to pray. Then the young infidel began to pull off his coat and get ready for bed. The uncle said, 'I thought you were going to sit up and watch.' But the young man knew there was no need of sitting up, pistol in hand, to watch all night long in a cabin that was hallowed by the word of God and consecrated by the voice of prayer."

The world owes more to the Book of books than human tongue can tell. Wherever the Bible goes, it carries with it life's choicest blessings. It is the maker of happy homes and peaceful communities. The Mosaic institutions are the foundation of the laws in civilized countries. The best that you find in literature is largely made up of jewels from this inexhaustible mine of truth. William J. Bryan, whose addresses often are studded with gems from the sacred Book, pays it this tribute: "Wherever the moral standard is being lifted up,—wherever life is becoming larger in the vision that directs it, and richer in its fruitage,—the improvement is traceable to the Bible, and to the influence of the God and Christ of whom the Bible tells."

From an educational standpoint, the Bible is the Book of books. Charles Dudley Warner, a great magazine writer, says: "A fair knowledge of the Bible is in itself almost a liberal education, as many great masters in literature have testified. It has so entered into law, literature, thought, the whole modern life of the Christian world, that ignorance of it is a most serious disadvantage to the student." Ruskin, the great art critic, tells, in his autobiography, how his mother "established his soul in life" by making him read and commit to memory large portions of the Bible. He says: "To this discipline, patient, accurate, and resolute, I owe much of my general power of taking pains, and the best part of my taste in literature. I count it, very confidently, the most precious, and, on the whole, the one essential part of my education."

It would seem that a book so thoroughly good, so essentially helpful, so unmistakably divine, could have no enemies. But, as H. L. Hastings said: "The Bible is a book which has been refuted, demolished, overthrown, and exploded more times than any other book you ever heard of. Every little while, somebody starts up and upsets this book; and it is like upsetting a solid cube of granite. It is just as big one way as the other; and when you have upset it, it is right side up; and when you overturn it again, it is right side up still. Every little while, somebody blows up the Bible; but when it comes down, it always lights on its feet, and runs faster than ever through the world."

Voltaire said, "The Bible is an exploded book." Thirty-two years ago, R. G. Ingersoll said, "In ten years, the Bible will not be read." So infidels have prophesied. They have attacked the word of God; but each time, they have broken their weapons on this great Gibraltar of truth. From every battle, God's Book comes forth victorious, and presses on to make new conquests. Every country in the world, with the exception of Tibet, Afghanistan, and some of the Mohammedan states of North Africa, is now open to the circulation of the Bible. Twenty-seven Bible societies are printing the Bible,—two in the United States, three in Great Britain, and twenty-two on the European continent. More copies of the Bible are sold annually than of any other one hundred books combined. Ten million Bibles in English are distributed every year.

Then why is it, with this wonderful Book of books in the hands of every Christian, that so few are living the life that counts?—Simply because the Bible is not studied and appreciated as it should be. Cut an army off from its supplies, and it must soon retreat. Cut a Christian off from his Bible, "the sword of the Spirit," and he is bound to be defeated in the conflict with the enemy. Our Master, when on earth, *knew* the Scriptures. He made them a part of His life; and He vanquished the enemy with, "It is written."

Jesus prayed, "Sanctify them through Thy truth: Thy word is truth;" and He commanded us to *"search* the Scriptures." At another time, He said, "Ye shall know the truth, and the truth shall make you free." A great general once ordered an iron armor. When it was brought, he asked, "Is it safe?" "Yes, sir," replied the messenger. "Then put it on, and let me test it," commanded the general. The armor that Christ asks us to put on has been tested. He wore it, and was safe; for He "was in all points tempted like as we are, yet without sin." Our only safety, in these troublous times, lies in an experimental knowledge of the Scriptures and an unbroken communion with Heaven.

No one can be a successful soul winner without being a Bible student. He must know his Guidebook. What would you think of a man posing as a guide, who did not know where to find the places of most interest to tourists? In order to be a good guide, you must also be a strong Christian. "Lean Christians," says one, "own Bibles, but feed on newspapers." Study your Bible, and study it with the determination to *live it.* The Word must *abide* in us. Yes, *read* your Bible; for "from the first chapter of Genesis onward, the whole Bible is, in symbol or in fact, a record of the victorious life, the delineation of what it is, the demonstration of how it can be lived." No matter what higher criticism says, he who reads the Bible sincerely, finds it still *quick* and *powerful*. Its words are fresh as the morning dew; and somehow, "they bring us to God, and they bring God to us, and form a means of communication by which we can live our life with and for God."

William Carey was a busy cobbler; but with the open Bible on one side of his bench, and a map of the world on the other, he found time to study the sinner's Guidebook and the heathen's need. Spurgeon said: "I should like to see a huge pile of all the books, good and bad, that were ever written, prayer books, and sermons, and hymn books, and all, smoking like Sodom of old, if the reading of these books keeps you away from the reading of the Bible; for a ton weight of human literature is not worth an ounce of Scripture. One single drop of the essential tincture of the word of God is better than a sea full of our commentings, and sermonizings, and the like."

My dear young friend, would you live the life that counts? Then you must be a Bible student—you must spend much time alone with God and His word. As you and I "try to become acquainted with our heavenly Father through His word, angels will draw near, our minds will be strengthened, our characters will be elevated and refined. We shall become more like our Saviour." Every young Christian, through faithful, prayerful Bible study, may say with the psalmist, "Thy word have I hid in mine heart, that I might not sin against Thee."

There are other reasons why you should study your Bible. In all the vicissitudes of life, that Book meets every need of the human heart; and every young Christian should know this for himself. In heathen lands or in civilized countries, in prisons or in palaces, in times of famine or in days of feasting, in poverty or in prosperity, that precious Book speaks to the human heart. When enjoying the comforts of peace or when suffering the calamities of war; while absorbed in the things of this world or while meditating on the glories of the next; when thrilling with exuberant health or when languishing on beds of sickness; when rejoicing over the cradle or when weeping over the grave; when doubt, perplexity, and fear struggle for possession, or when pleasure, wealth, and popularity lead to forgetfulness,—yes, under all circumstances, as many have testified, the Book of God has a message for the human heart—just the message it needs.

And you should study your Bible because it will inspire you with courage and determination to press on. The men and women on its pages are so human! They did not always succeed; sometimes they, too, failed. The Bible record shows us how patiently and sympathetically God deals with His erring children, and it reminds us that "He knoweth *our* frame; He remembereth that *we* are dust." How comforting it is to know that the Father understands me! And I *know* He does; for the pages of His Book mirror my own heart, and meet its hidden needs. Why should we not study the Book that tells of God's wonderful love, of His constant care, and of His unquenchable desire to save us?

But I think there is no stronger reason for urging you to spend much time with the Book of books than this: It will make Jesus more real to you than any earthly friend. He is always near. He always has time to visit.

There is nothing you cannot talk over with Him; and He always understands, sympathizes, and gives the counsel needed. You and I may have Him walk so close beside us that He can hear our thoughts and feel our heartaches. He is the one Friend we can always keep. He is the one Friend we cannot spare; for truly, as He has said, "Without Me ye can do nothing." He is the one Friend through whom you and I can do all things we should do to be true Christians; and the Bible is the book that will bring Him into our lives and make Him the closest and most real of all friends.

Do you not love the Bible? If you do not, there is only one explanation: You do not know the Book. You have not been drinking deeply enough of its living waters to wash the dust of common things out of your throat. Drink deeply, and you will long for it as the "hart panteth after the water brooks." Drink deeply, and you will seek it as the desert traveler seeks the cooling spring. Drink deeply, and you will find it the panacea for all human needs.

> Thy word is everlasting truth.
>   How pure is every page!
> Thy holy Book shall guide my youth,
>   And well support my age.
>   — *Isaac Watts.*

*T*ake Time to Be Holy

Take time to be holy. Speak oft with thy Lord;
Abide in Him always, and feed on His word;
Make friends of God's children; help those who
    are weak,
Forgetting in nothing His blessing to seek.

Take time to be holy. The world rushes on;
Spend much time in secret with Jesus alone.
By looking to Jesus, like Him thou shalt be;
Thy friends in thy conduct His likeness shall see.

Take time to be holy. Let Him be thy Guide,
And run not before Him, whatever betide;
In joy or in sorrow, still follow thy Lord,
And looking to Jesus, still trust in His word.

Take time to be holy. Be calm in thy soul,
Each thought and each motive beneath His control.
Thus led by His Spirit to fountains of love,
Thou soon shalt be fitted for service above.

                         — *W. D. Longstaff.*

Take Time to Pray

"Pray without ceas-
ing." 1 Thess. 5: 17.

"Be not too busy with thy work and care
To look to God, to clasp thy hand in His.
Miss thou all else, but fail not thou of this.
Thou need'st not all alone thy burdens bear;
Listen and wait, obey and learn His will,
His love and service all thy life shall fill."

CHAPTER VI

THE great freight and passenger trains are never too busy to stop for coal and water. No matter how congested the yards may be, no matter how crowded the schedules are, no matter how many things demand the attention of the trainmen, those trains *always stop* for coal and water. But why do they spend time stopping for coal and water when there is so much to do?—Oh, those men *know* they cannot run without these supplies. Coal and water are the source of power. The trains just *must take time* to be supplied with power. If they did not, the railroad traffic would be tied up. "Dead engines" with their trains would be strewn along the road, and traveling would be not only dangerous, but impossible. So the trains *take time* to be supplied with

(71)

power enough for efficient service. But have
you ever stopped to think how seriously the
work of God's church is blockaded by the
"dead" Christians who are not willing to stop
long enough to get power from God to serve
Him acceptably?

When General Gordon was in Africa, he
was very busy; but he found time to pray.
Every morning, there was spread outside of
his tent a handkerchief, to remind the soldiers
that their general was having an interview
with the great General of heaven and earth.

One morning, some friends called to see a
Christian business man. Their errand seemed
urgent. The clerk said, "You cannot see him
now." "But we must." Finally the clerk
yielded, and saying, "I will show you where
he is," led the way back into the storeroom
among the boxes. There in that quiet, secluded part of the store was the business man.
He was on his knees praying, and before him
lay an open Bible.

Of George Washington's private religious
habits, his nephew, Robert Lewis, says: "I
accidentally witnessed Washington's private
devotions in his library, both morning and
evening. On these occasions, I saw him in
a kneeling posture, with a Bible open be-

fore him." Another writer adds: "When Mrs. Washington's sixteen-year-old daughter, Martha Custis, lay dying at Mount Vernon, Washington knelt beside her, and tearfully prayed that her life might be spared. At Valley Forge, Washington was frequently seen to retire to a secluded grove. Mr. Potts, a Quaker, followed him on one occasion, and saw him on his knees in prayer. He returned, and told his family he was sure the American cause would prevail, because he had seen the American commander in prayer."

Never was prayer needed more than it is just now. And truly, as S. D. Gordon says in "Quiet Talks on Prayer":

"The great people of the earth to-day are the people who pray,—people who take time to pray. They have not time. It must be taken from something else. That something else is important, very important and pressing, but still, less important and pressing than prayer. There are people who put prayer first, and group the other items in life's schedule around and after prayer. These are the people to-day who are doing the most for God; in winning souls; in solving problems; in awakening churches; in supplying both men and money for mission posts; in keeping fresh and strong their lives far off in sacrificial service on the foreign field, where the thickest fighting is going on; in keeping the old earth sweet a little while longer."

Prayer is the most important factor in Christian life; for the Christian's *first* duty is, rightly to represent his Master to others— to live the life that counts; and prayer is the breath of the life that counts. Some one tells a story of a young artist who desired to copy a beautiful picture that hung in a palace. He could not obtain permission to copy it in the palace, so he determined to reproduce it from memory. Hour after hour, he would sit and gaze at the picture, until it took possession of him. Then he would hurry to his studio, and begin to paint. Each day, he spent some time gazing on the original. As he gazed and studied and toiled, his power grew. Finally there hung in his studio such a wonderful copy, that all who saw it said, "We must see the original." It should be the object of all our Christian service, to represent our Saviour so well that men will say, "We must see Jesus." Time spent gazing upon Him is not lost. By beholding, we become changed. The more time we spend with Him, the more we shall grow to be like Him.

There is another reason why prayer is the most important factor in Christian life, and that is that prayer is the greatest power on earth for winning souls. Of his conversion, Hudson Taylor says: "One day, which I shall never forget, when I was about fifteen years old, my dear mother being absent from home some eighty miles away, I had a holiday. I searched through the library for a book to while away time. I selected a gospel tract which looked attractive, saying: 'There will be an interesting story at the commencement, and a sermon or a moral at the end. I will take the former, and leave the latter for those who like it.' I little knew what was going on in the heart of my dear mother. She arose from the dinner table with an intense yearning for the conversion of her boy, and feeling that, being from home, and having more leisure than she otherwise would, there was a special opportunity afforded her of pleading with God for me. She went to her bedroom, turned the key in the door, and resolved not to leave the room until her prayers were answered. Hour after hour did that dear mother plead for me, until she could praise God for the conversion of her son. In the meantime, as I was reading the tract, 'The Finished Work of

Christ,' a light was flashed into my soul by the
Holy Spirit, that there was nothing to be done
but to fall on my knees and accept this Saviour
and His salvation, and praise God forevermore. While my mother was praising God in
her closet, I was praising Him in the old warehouse where I had retired to read my book.
When I met mother at the door, on her return, with the glad news, she said: 'I know,
my boy; I have been rejoicing for a fortnight
in the glad tidings you have to tell me.' "

"Up in a little town in Maine," said Dr.
Torrey, in an address, "things were pretty
dead some years ago. The churches were not
accomplishing anything. There were a few
godly men in the churches, and they said:
'Here we are, only uneducated laymen; but
something must be done in this town. Let us
form a praying band. We will all center our
prayers on one man. Who shall it be?' They
picked out one of the hardest men in town, a
hopeless drunkard, and centered all their
prayers upon him. In a week, he was converted. They centered their prayers upon the
next hardest man in town, and soon he was
converted. Then they took up another and
another, until within a year, two or three hundred were brought to God, and the fire spread

out into all the surrounding country. Definite prayer for those in the prison house of sin is the need of the hour."

All service should begin in prayer, and be saturated with prayer; for prayer dissolves difficulties. After good evangelistic meetings in a California college, some one said to a young man who had been much troubled over certain questions of faith, "Your difficulties don't seem very important, do they?" His face beamed with heavenly joy as he answered, "They're all gone." Yes, prayer always is doing the impossible things in the world.

During the early history of the theological seminary at Alleghany, the institute was frequently in financial straits. "One time, when it was in great need of funds, and had reached a very trying monetary extremity, Dr. Herron, the president of the board of directors, called a meeting of the board. There were only three in attendance, including the president himself. Dr. Herron, Dr. Swift, and Dr. Patterson composed the council. Dr. Herron expressed it as his opinion that unless immediate financial assistance arrived, the further perpetuation of the institution was impossible. 'Oh,' he said, in a very discouraged tone of voice, 'we have no one to help

us.' 'No one to help us?' repeated Dr. Patterson. 'Why, I know of a thousand.' 'A
thousand!' exclaimed Dr. Herron. 'I do not
understand.   I wish you would explain.'
'Well, the explanation is this,' replied Dr.
Patterson: 'I am a cipher, Dr. Swift is a
cipher, and you are a cipher; but Jesus Christ
is a unit, and my mathematical education
teaches me that a unit with three ciphers on
the right side make a thousand. So I know
of a thousand who are ready and willing to
help. And as man's extremity is God's opportunity, let us pray.' They prayed; help
came; help remained. The seminary was en-
dowed; and from the directors' prayer meeting to the present time, few financial disturb-
ances have interfered with the prosperity of
the institution. Thank God for the power
and the utility of prayer."

Yet, in the face of these and innumerable
other facts, showing plainly that "prayer is
the greatest force in God's great world," men
and women, Christian men and women, men
and women who declare stoutly that they believe these facts, say they cannot find time to
pray. "I have only made one New Year's
resolution," said a busy housewife; "I have
resolved to take time, through this new year,

to be holy." But, says William T. McElveen, in the *Advance* for March 6, 1913: "For the American to meditate is most difficult. He has little time to muse. The world is with him too late and too soon. He doesn't think that he is traveling unless he is going at the rate of sixty miles an hour. He lives in a delectable pell-mell and carnival of hurry. He has no leisure to brood."

"Too tired to pray! O Father, tired of toiling,
　Tired of the heavy load, the blistering way,
Weary of all the monotone of moiling,
　Tired out — too tired to pray!

"Too sad to pray! Undone, my God, with trouble,
　The same dull heartache borne another day,
My life an empty field of worthless rubble,
　And I — too sad to pray!

"Too sinful — yes, for any further praying,
　Too proud to hear, too wicked to obey,
Loathing the desert path, yet ever straying,
　And gone too far to pray!

"O Christ, pray for me! Weary, sad, in silence,
　My impotence at Thy dear feet I lay.
Jesus, my final Help, my All-Reliance,
　Pray — for I cannot pray."

How often, in our hustle, we forget to put first things first! As G. H. Knight says: "What we need above all things, in these crowded days, is the setting apart of many listening times, times of quiet, in which we can hear the heavenly voices that call to us unregarded in the busy day. . . . God has something to say to us which, in the whir of our earthly ambitions, we cannot hear; and He makes the noises of the outer world to cease, that He may speak to the soul. Sometimes He tries us in the night; sometimes He giveth songs in the night; but all these we shall utterly miss if there is no quiet time in which He can come very near to us. There are many ways of preparing to receive blessings from on high; but one of the most essential is this: 'Commune with your own heart, and be still.' "

Taking time to listen is an important part of prayer. We often are so practical in temporal things, and so impractical in religious matters! Often we tell God hurriedly of a hundred different things, and rush off before He has time to respond in any way. We do not wrestle, we do not *pray through* into the Master's presence, where He can speak peace to our troubled hearts. Our prayers must often seem like mockery to Him. Phillips Brooks tells of a little boy whom he saw struggling to ring a doorbell that was too high for him to reach. Out of sympathy, he stepped up to help the little lad. As soon as the bell rang, the mischievous little fellow turned his roguish eyes up to Mr. Brooks, and said, "Now, let's scoot." There was nothing for Mr. Brooks to do but to apologize for the little mischief-maker. I wonder sometimes how often our Mediator has to apologize for our rushing away without taking time to listen. F. B. Myers once said he always spent about fifteen minutes after prayer and Bible study just listening; and his testimony was that in that time of quiet meditation, "God has never failed to give me a program for the day."

In God's great universe, He knows no haste and no delays. He takes time to change the fields of waving green into ripened wheat. He takes time to paint the rose. And He wants to take time to make your life perfect, beautiful, and holy, like His own. He is willing to give *His* time, but you must also give *your* time in order for Him to do the work. Our Saviour, when on earth, *took time to pray.* (Matt. 14: 23; 26: 36, 39; Mark 1: 35; Luke 9: 18.) "Therefore," as R. F. Horton says, "whether the desire for prayer is on you or not, get to your closet at the set time; shut yourself in with God; wait upon Him; seek His face; realize Him; pray."

For young Christians, it is well to have some devotional helps for the hour of secret prayer. The Morning Watch Calendar, prepared for this special purpose, is excellent help. Do systematic reading in the Bible, and have a written prayer list of persons and things. S. D. Gordon gives the following valuable suggestions: (1) "Guard jealously a quiet, unhurried spirit. (2) Remember you have come to meet the Master—come to know Him better, to hear His voice, to realize His presence, to look into His face. (3) Your chief business is listening. (4) Give His Book first place in your trysting hour. (5) Be frank and honest with the Master as His Book points out sins."

Time spent alone with God is not wasted. It changes us; it changes our surroundings; and every young Christian who would live the life that counts, and who would have power for service, *must take time to pray.*

Lord, what a change within us one short hour
  Spent in Thy presence will suffice to make!
  What heavy burdens from our bosoms take!
What parched grounds revive, as with a shower!
We kneel, and all around us seems to lower;
  We rise, and all, the distant and the near,
  Stands forth a sunny outline brave and clear.
We kneel, how weak! We rise, how full of power!
  Why, therefore, should we do ourselves this wrong,
  Or others, that we are not always strong;

That we are ever overborne with care;
That we should ever weak or heartless be,
Anxious or troubled, when with us is prayer,
And joy and strength and courage are with Thee!

— *Trench.*

The Silent Hour

When the cold, gray dawn is breaking,
And the birds to song are waking,
    When the morn is robed in beauty,
        In the freshness of its flower,—
Then, before the fevered flurry,
Then, before the care and worry,
    Ere the labor of thy duty,
        Give thy soul a silent hour!

In the haven of His quiet,
Lose the world and all its riot!
    He hath love and joy and gladness,
        Sunshine when the shadows lower;
So, within the silent even,
Be thou lifted up to heaven,
    And no shadowing of sadness
        Shall molest thy silent hour!

Go thy way! Thy soul is stronger!
Thou canst strive and struggle longer
    For that brief yet glorious vision
        Of thy Father's promised power.
Wouldst thou have the fabled mixture
Of the magic life's elixir?—
    Find it in the realms elysian,
        In the mystic silent hour!

— *Llewellyn A. Wilcox.*

Pray Without Ceasing

Unanswered yet, the prayer your lips have pleaded
  In agony of heart, these many years?
Does faith begin to fail, is hope declining,
  And think you all in vain those falling tears?
Say not the Father has not heard your prayer.
You shall have your desire, sometime, somewhere.

Unanswered yet, though when you first presented
  This one petition at the Father's throne,
It seemed you could not wait the time of asking,
  So anxious was your heart to have it done?
If years have passed since then, do not despair,
For God will answer you sometime, somewhere.

Unanswered yet? But you are not unheeded.
  The promises of God *forever* stand.
To Him, our days and years alike are equal.
  "*Have faith in God.*" It is your Lord's command.
Hold on to Jacob's angel, and your prayer
Shall bring a blessing down sometime, somewhere.

Unanswered yet? Nay, do not say unanswered.
  Perhaps your part is not yet wholly done.
The work began when first your prayer was uttered,
  And God will finish what He has begun.
Keep incense burning at the shrine of prayer,
And *glory* shall descend, sometime, somewhere.

Unanswered yet? Faith cannot be unanswered.
  Her feet are firmly planted on the Rock.
Amid the wildest storm, she stands undaunted,
  Nor quails before the loudest thunder shock.
She knows *Omnipotence* has heard her prayer,
And cries, "It shall be done, sometime, somewhere."
                              — *Mrs. F. G. Burroughs.*

Essentials to Successful Prayer Life

"Lord, teach us to
pray." Luke 11:1.

God answers prayer. Sometimes, when hearts are weak,
He gives the very gifts believers seek.
  But often faith must learn a deeper rest,
And trust God's silence when He does not speak;
  For He whose name is Love will send the best.
  Stars may burn out, nor mountain walls endure;
  But God is true. His promises are sure
To those who seek.

— *Plantz.*

CHAPTER VII

THE young Christian who would live the life that counts, who would be equipped for successful service, must not only spend much time alone with God in prayer, but must make the most of this supreme privilege. One writer says, "The stigma upon Christian life is the unholy content without any distinct experiences of answers to prayer."

In all business relations, one must meet the conditions, in order to reap the results. The same law obtains in prayer. "Most prayers are not answered, and yet God fulfills His promises. The cause of this recognized failure, then, must be in the failure to fulfill con-

ditions." The spirit of Christ must enter into
every true prayer, and true prayer is always
answered. "If our prayers are not answered,"
says D. L. Moody, "it may be that we have
prayed without the right motive, or that we
have not prayed according to the Scriptures."
Let us see what the elements of true prayer
are as revealed in the Bible and in the experiences of others. If you feel that prayer is
a failure, perhaps it is because some of these
elements are missing in your own petitions.

1. Adoration

Do you adore the God upon whom you call
for daily blessings? The centurion and the
Syrophœnician woman recognized His supe-
riority. Some one has said truly, "If we *know*
Christ, we cannot be proud; if we *know* ourselves, we must be humble."

2. Thanksgiving

How much thanksgiving do you mix in with
your prayers? Paul says, "In everything by
prayer and supplication *with thanksgiving*
let your requests be made known unto God."
If Christians would spend more time thanking
God for His wonderful goodness to the children of men, they would have little time or
disposition to murmur or complain.

The old farmer kneeling at a soldier's grave near Nashville leaves us a good example of gratitude. Some one asked him: "Why do you pay so much attention to this grave? Was your son buried there?" "No," said he. "During the war, my family were all sick. I knew not how to leave them. I was drafted. One of my neighbors came over and said: 'I will go for you; I have no family.' He went. He was wounded in the Chickamauga. He was carried to the hospital, and there he died. And, sir, I have come a great many miles that I might write over his grave these words: *He died for me.*"

The Saviour died for you and me. After His resurrection, He went to heaven to plead the sinner's case. Every day, He is pleading our cases before the heavenly court; every day, He is sending His angels to guard us, and the Holy Spirit to teach us; every day, He is showering upon us the manifold blessings of life. Surely our hearts should overflow with gratitude, our daily lives should be a constant expression of genuine appreciation of His wonderful goodness, and our prayers should be saturated with praise and thanksgiving.

3. Confession

Do you confess to Him your sins in the spirit of true penitence? Daniel, the greatly beloved, classed himself with his people, and seven times, in his prayer, he confessed offenses of which they were guilty. Notice the prayers of Job, David, the publican. These were all uttered in the spirit of humility. Not so with Pharaoh's prayer that the plagues be stayed, or the Pharisee's proud announcement that he was not like other men. Thomas Fuller says that man's owning his own weakness is the only stock onto which God can graft the grace of His assistance. Humility and confession must characterize the prayer that does not fail. God has promised to answer the prayer of the humble. (2 Chron. 7: 14.)

4. Restitution

So far as lies in your power, have you tried to make restitution wherever you have wronged others? Zaccheus did. A writer commenting on Zaccheus, gives the following illustration of restitution: "Sultan Selymus could tell his counselor Pyrrhus, who persuaded him to bestow the great wealth he had taken from the Persian merchants upon some notable hospital for the relief of the poor, that God hates robbery for burnt offering. The dying Turk commanded it rather be restored to the right owners, which was done accordingly, to the great shame of many Christians, who mind nothing less than they do restitution."

5. FORGIVENESS

Did you ever ask God to forgive you for an offense while you were harboring in your heart a grudge against some one else? And did you expect Him to be so inconsistent as to do it?

"I believe," says D. L. Moody, in speaking on this subject, "this is keeping more people from having power with God than any other thing; they are not willing to cultivate a spirit of forgiveness. . . . When you go into the door of God's kingdom, you go in through the door of forgiveness. I never knew a man to get a blessing into his own soul if he was not willing to forgive others." If we pray according to His will, we will pray in a forgiving spirit, with a heart that harbors no grudge; for He has taught us to say, "Forgive us our debts, *as* we forgive our debtors." The prayer of the unforgiving heart is bound to fail.

6. FAITH

We are told by James to "ask in faith, nothing wavering"; for says he of the one who wavers, "Let not that man think that he shall receive anything of the Lord." Mere words do not constitute prayer. A picture of a fire is not a fire; a description of Niagara Falls is not the falls. So-called "prayer," says Bishop Hall, "if it is only dribbled from careless lips, falls at our feet." To form words into prayer—into the effectual prayer that pierces the clouds above, and reaches the throne of heaven—takes faith; but every child of God may pray the "effectual prayer that availeth much." Prayer without faith is like a check without a signature. It is worthless; for the signature below is what gives a check value. But the prayer *of faith* has on it the signature of the Lord Jesus Christ, and is good for any amount when presented at the bank of heaven. (Phil. 4:19.)

A little mountain village had been amply and regularly supplied with water from a lake above; but one morning, the housewives opened the faucets in vain. There was a little noise, but no water. The pipe connecting the village with the lake was carefully examined.

No break was found; nothing seemed wrong; yet no water came, and the villagers despaired. Some moved away. But one day, one of the town officials received a note. It said: "Ef you'll jes pull de plug out from de top, you'll get all de water you want." The plug was removed, there was an abundance of water, and prosperity returned to the half-famished, half-deserted village.

How many Christians are robbing themselves of heaven's blessings in just this way! They pray; but the channel through which the blessing must come is plugged with *unbelief*. Asking and not believing is like holding a well corked bottle under a faucet to be filled. Read these words from "Desire of Ages": "It is faith that connects us with heaven and brings us strength for coping with the powers of darkness. In Christ, God has provided means for subduing every sinful trait, and resisting every temptation, however strong." And again, from the same author: "The grace of God comes to the soul through the channel of living faith, and that faith it is in our power to exercise. True faith lays hold of and claims the promised blessing before it is realized and felt. We must send up our petitions *in faith* within the second veil, and let faith take hold of the promised blessing and claim it as ours."

Faith brings the resources of heaven within reach of the humblest petitioner; and the sad thing is that there seems to be so little of it among Christians. Most Christians exercise faith freely in temporal things. For instance, you go to a railroad ticket office. You buy a ticket, and hand over to the agent your money in exchange for a piece of paper that will take you to your destination. You do not fret and worry, and keep wondering if it will take you there. You have confidence in the railroad company. You go to the dining room, and there unbelief does not seem to trouble you; you eat, definitely expecting your food to nourish you. What must God think of us when we look up to our never failing Friend with distrust and unbelief stamped upon our hearts?

When Christ came down from the Mount of Transfiguration, and the perplexed father cried to him, "If Thou canst do anything, have compassion on us, and help us," Jesus replied, "If thou canst believe, all things are possible to him that believeth." That is exactly what He says to you and to me. And shall we not cry, with that Galilean petitioner,

"Lord, I believe; help Thou mine unbelief"? As Cortland Myers says: "If we could only look behind the curtains, we would be able to trace the streams of power back to their source in the heavens. We would discern that the very instant the *prayer* of *faith* was uttered in the secret silence of the lonely soul, there was something taking place at the other end of the line, and in other lines, and in other parts of the world."

This absolute faith in God which is needed to carry our petitions to the court room above, is a most wonderful transformer of human life. It lifts one above worry. It gives to life a buoyancy that is a tonic to others. It inspires others just as the pipers did the Highlanders. History tells us that during the battle of Waterloo, Wellington discovered that the valiant forty-second Highlanders were wavering. Immediately the pipers were called into the firing line. When those Scotch heroes heard the first strains of that martial music, they rallied; the lines were quickly re-formed; and with a wild cheer, they swept the field before them. Even so our faith should help to inspire others to be victorious in the battle of life.

Then, too, absolute faith in God, in His personal care for you, gives that wonderful peace which pleasure, prosperity, fame, or anything else cannot give; neither can sorrow, poverty, nor trouble take it away. The faith of Paul and Silas had ripened into perfect trustfulness as they sang praises to God in the prison dungeon, with iron shackles on their feet. Truly, as Isaiah says, "Thou wilt keep him in perfect peace, whose mind is stayed on Thee: because he trusteth in Thee."

7. Obedience

The promise is, "If ye abide in Me, and My words abide in you, ye shall ask what ye will, and it shall be done unto you." John 15: 7. "Faith must have for its companion, obedience. Faith never walks alone the path that leads to the heart of God." Rather, obedience is the invariable fruit of faith. It is the "obedience of faith."

Several years ago, I attended the International Student Volunteer Convention. There were present, at the first meeting, about five thousand student delegates from the colleges and universities in the United States and Canada. John R. Mott, in his opening address, spoke of the importance of that great gathering. One sentence in that address, I think I never shall forget: "The most obscure delegate in this great convention may hinder us from getting the appointed blessing."

Even so, the most obscure *known* sin hidden in the heart of any Christian will hinder him from living the life that counts. The terrible thing about little pet sins is that they do not stay little; they are bound to grow, and ruin the life. Some one has said, "Every indulgence is a waste pipe by which we let life run into the gutter." The heart that harbors *known* sin cannot get into close touch with God, for sin is an insulator. It breaks one's connection with heaven. He who would pray well must endeavor to live well. There is but one prayer for the heart with known sin in it, and that is, "Cleanse me." Clinging to sin makes praying, effectual praying, impossible; for "praying is working with God; sin is working against God."

What would you think if a friend, after repeatedly urging you to call, should lock the door each time you came near, and refuse to let you in? Very soon you would say, "Well, he doesn't want me to come, even though he keeps on asking me." That is just the way some of us treat the Holy Spirit. We want

His *power* in our lives, but we are unwilling to give Him the right of way. We *must* learn that we cannot use the Holy Spirit; we are to let Him use us.

God can use any kind of vessel, large or small, metal or wooden; but it must be *clean;* so, naturally, the first thing the Holy Spirit does when He is called to enter a human heart, is to begin to clean up the life. He points out wrong things in it. He puts His finger on that pet sin, and says, "This must be cast out." If a person had a malignant cancer, and the surgeon should say, "The only thing that will save your life is an operation," you would consider the patient extremely foolish to refuse to have the operation. Yet when the divine Surgeon comes to cut cherished sins out of our lives in order to save us, how many say: "Oh, I never can give those up! It seems to me I have to give up so much more than any one else!"

Yes, it will seem so. *Living Waters* says: "If God has called you to be really like Jesus, He will draw you into a life of crucifixion and humility, and put upon you such demands of obedience, that you will not be able to follow other people, or measure yourself by other Christians, and in many ways He *will seem* to let other good people do things which He will not let you do. Settle it forever, then, that you are to deal directly with God, and that He is to have the privilege of tying your tongue, or chaining your hand, or closing your eyes, in ways that He does not seem to use with others. Now when you are so possessed with the living God that you are, in your secret heart, pleased and delighted over this peculiar, personal, private, jealous guardianship and management of the Holy Spirit over your life, you will have found the vestibule of heaven."

"Faith has no desire to have its own will, when that will is not in accordance with the mind of God," says Spurgeon; "for such a desire would at bottom be the impulse of an unbelief which did not rely on God's judgment as our best guide. Faith knows that God's will is the highest good, and that anything which is beneficial to us will be granted to our petitions." One day, a woman who was very sick was asked whether she desired to live or to die. She replied, "Which God pleases." "But," asked another, "if God should refer it to you, which would you choose?" "Truly," came back the answer, "I would refer it to Him again." Fenelon, too, was anxious to obey the divine will; for he prayed, "O God, take my heart, for I cannot give it; and when Thou hast it, keep it, for I cannot keep it for Thee; and save me in spite of myself."

Every young Christian should pray, with Fenelon, to be made willing to obey His will in all things—always to say, "Thy will be done." If obedience brings suffering and sacrifice, remember, in the words of Dyer: "Afflictions are blessings to us when we can bless God for afflictions. Suffering has kept many from sinning. God had one Son without sin, but He never had any without sorrow. Fiery trials make golden Christians; sanctified afflictions are spiritual promotions."

Rutherford exclaimed: "Oh, what owe I to the file, to the hammer, to the furnace of my Lord Jesus, who hath now let me see how good the wheat of Christ is that goeth through His mill and His oven to be made into bread for His own table! Grace tried is better than grace; it is more than grace; it is glory in its infancy. Oh, how little getteth Christ of us, but that which He winneth with much toil and pains! And how soon would faith freeze without a cross! . . . Why should I start at the plow of my Lord, that maketh deep furrows on my soul? I know that He is no idle husbandman; He purposeth a crop."

If you are determined to be an "extraordinary Christian," and be able to prevail with God in prayer, and with men in service, you must not grieve the Holy Spirit, but give Him the right of way. The hands that are lifted up in prayer for power must be clean; the arms that are stretched out to save men must not be broken. David exclaimed, "The Lord rewarded me according to my righteousness: according to the cleanness of my hands hath He recompensed me." 2 Sam. 22:21. Cortland Myers puts it in this way: "The name of Jesus must be the ruling power in life in order to be the ruling power in prayer." This sounds almost like slavery; but it is not, in the harsh sense of the term; it is slipping into the care and guidance of Him who *loved* us so much that He died to save us. And we may be sure that He will ask us to give up only those things which hurt or hinder our life, and,—

"Sometime, when all life's lessons we have learned,
　And sun and stars forevermore have set,
The things which our weak judgments here have spurned,
　The things o'er which we've grieved with lashes wet,
Will flash before us, out of earth's dark night,
　As stars shine most in deepest tints of blue,
And we shall see how all God's plans were right,
　And what we deemed reproof was love most true."

8. DEFINITENESS

A young minister came to Spurgeon lamenting the fact that so few were led to Christ under his preaching. "But," said Spurgeon, "you don't expect some one to accept Christ in every service, do you?" "Oh, no, of course not," said the young man. "Well," continued Spurgeon, "that is just why you are failing." We must not only "attempt great things for God," and "expect great things from Him," but we must be definite in our requests. The majority of our prayers are so general that we do not know whether they are answered or not.

Dr. J. G. K. McClure tells of an invalid woman residing in Springfield, Illinois, who had been bedridden for seventeen years, and was almost helpless. For many years, she had been praying to God in a general way to save souls. One day, she asked for pen and paper. She wrote down the names of fifty-seven acquaintances. She prayed for each of them by name three times a day. She wrote them letters of her interest in them. She also wrote to Christian friends in whom she knew these persons had confidence, and urged them to speak to these persons about their soul's welfare, and do their best to persuade them to repent and believe. She had unquestioning faith in God. In her humble, earnest dependence upon Him, she thus interceded for the unsaved. In time, every one of these fifty-seven persons avowed faith in Jesus Christ as his personal Saviour.

Perhaps you are familiar with the story of the boy soul winner in England. After this little boy had passed away, they opened a small box he had kept with other treasures, and found in it a list of forty boys. The first one was his seat mate at the time he went to the pastor and asked for something to do for the Lord, and the last name was Neddie Smith. And every boy on the list was converted. He had taken them one by one in faith and prayer, giving them books to read, showing them texts of Scripture, praying with and for them till the Lord awakened them, and the whole forty had been converted through his efforts.

Shortly after the Civil War, D. L. Moody was holding meetings in one of the Southern cities. One night, a man came to him weeping and trembling. Mr. Moody says: "I thought something I had said had aroused him, and I began to question him as to what it was. I found, however, he could not tell a word of what I had said. 'My friend,' said I, 'what is the trouble?' He put his hand in his pocket, and brought out a letter, all soiled, as if his tears had fallen on it. 'I got that letter,' he said, 'from my sister last night. She tells me that every night, she goes to her knees and prays to God for me. I think I am the worst man in all the Army of the Cumberland. I have been perfectly wretched to-day.' That sister was six hundred miles away; yet she had brought her brother to his knees in answer to her earnest, believing prayer. It was a hard case; but God heard and answered the prayer of this godly sister, so that the man was as clay in the hands of the potter. He was soon brought into the kingdom of God—all through his sister's prayers."

Stop a moment, and look upon your own prayers. How many *definite* things are you pleading with God for day after day? Notice some of the wonderful prayers in the Bible: Jacob wrestled with God all night, pleading with Him to soften Esau's heart, and the brothers were reconciled. (Gen. 32: 24-30.) Elijah asked that the heavens be closed, and

for three and one half years no rain fell.
(James 5: 17.)   Elisha prayed for the dead
child, and it was restored to life.   (2 Kings
4: 33-35.)   Jehoahaz prayed that Israel be
freed from the yoke of Syria; God heard his
cry, and sent a deliverer.   (2 Kings 13: 4.)
Hezekiah's prayer for deliverance from Sen-
nacherib's army was answered.   (2 Kings 19:
20.)   Jabez made a definite request of God,
and the record says it was granted. (1 Chron.
4: 10.)   Asa's prayer brought deliverance
from the Ethiopians.   (2 Chron. 14: 11, 12.)
Read Jehoshaphat's prayer recorded in 2
Chron. 20: 6-17.

The prayers of Manasseh, Ezra, Nehemiah,
Job, David, Jeremiah, Daniel, the blind man,
the thief on the cross, Cornelius, and many
others, show the importance of being definite.
In fact, how do you know that your prayers
are not answered, if you are making no definite requests?   D. L. Moody says: "Our
prayers go all around the world without anything definite being asked for.   We do not
expect anything.   Many people would be
greatly surprised if God did answer their
prayers."   Do not forget that while not all
definite prayers are answered, all answered
prayers on record were definite.

9. Perseverance

The world is strewn with men and women who are failures because they lacked perseverance in pursuit of some chosen goal. Much money has been wasted in good oil fields and in mines rich in ore, because the prospectors gave up too soon. Cyrus W. Field refused to give up, and he brought two continents within speaking distance. Regardless of all obstacles, and even though the crew threatened to kill him, Columbus each day wrote in his diary, "And this day we sailed westward, as our course was." His perseverance brought to Europe's millions a new world of opportunity. For several months, Edison toiled to get his phonograph to say "Specia." It persisted in saying "Pecia," "pecia." But finally he conquered.

Perseverance always wins. The men and women who have prayed without ceasing, not only have had their prayers answered, but have enriched the world and lifted it spiritually. George Müller prayed for the conversion of three friends; and he said he knew they would become Christians, for he was going to pray till they did. Livingstone died upon his knees, and he opened a continent for the gospel. "Over a hundred years ago, a number of students in Yale University rose each morning before daybreak, and through the long winter months, pleaded with God for a revival. The revival came, and it is said that every student in the university surrendered to Christ."

A Christian woman in England had an unconverted husband. She was anxious that he should accept Christ as his personal Saviour. Her husband had forbidden her to speak to him on the subject; but she knew she could take his case to God, and she did. She said to herself, "I am going to pray for his conversion every day for twelve months." Every day, she went alone with God, and pleaded for the conversion of her husband. When the year was up, he had not yielded, neither did he show any signs of being under conviction. She said, "I am going to keep on six months longer." She did. Still there was no change. Should she give up?—"No," she said, "I will pray for him as long as God gives me breath." That very day, the answer came. Her husband came home to dinner, but instead of eating, he retired to his room. After she had waited a long time for him, she went to learn what detained him. There he was on his knees, pleading with God for mercy. He was thoroughly converted, and became a splendid Christian worker. This woman sought and found; asked and received; knocked, and it was opened unto her; for she knocked until the answer came.

Let every young Christian be equally persevering in asking favors of God. It will be well to keep a written prayer list, and check off each item as God answers your request concerning it. Let us test our petitions by His word, subject them to His will, and then keep them spread before Him until the answer comes. And let us know for ourselves that "that is the sublimest moment in human life which holds on by faith to God's promises with a deathless grip."

Sometimes God answers immediately. Daniel's prayer was answered at once. (Dan. 7: 19, 23.) Sometimes the answer is delayed; and then we may be sure the delay is for our best good. The earnest, sincere prayer is never unheard, and never left unanswered; for "shall not God avenge His own elect, which cry day and night unto Him?" Luke 18: 7, 8. Sometimes God's answer is different from what the petitioner expects. Three times, Paul prayed for deliverance from a thorn in the flesh; but God said "No," and Paul then gloried in that refusal. God gave him something better than he asked. Often God's answer is far beyond the expectation of His praying child. "Call unto Me," is God's message to you, "and I will answer thee, and show thee great and mighty things, which thou knowest not." Jer. 33: 3. David says, "I waited *patiently* for the Lord; and He inclined unto me, and heard my cry." Ps. 40: 1.

And He will answer you, if you too *wait patiently* for Him in the spirit of persevering prayer.

Pray without ceasing. Christ did. He lived in the atmosphere of prayer. Never give up. Christ wants to enter your heart, to repeat His victory in your life, His miracles in your work; but you must keep the connection unbroken.

10. SUBMISSION

Lastly, our prayers must always be made in the spirit of "Thy will be done." Sometimes we spread before God His promises, but cover up the conditions on which they are fulfilled. Isaiah tells us, "The Lord's hand is not shortened, that it cannot save; neither His ear heavy, that it cannot hear." This is where we often stop, and say, "God must fulfill this promise." But the prophet does not stop there. He adds this strong negative clause: "But your iniquities have separated between you and your God; and your sins have hid His face from you, that He will not hear." David said, "If I regard iniquity in my heart, the Lord will not hear me." Where there is a lack of submission, prayers are very liable to be selfish. We ask for blessings not for His glory, not for the good of others, but for selfish gratification. Is there not a lesson for us in the experience of Job? We read that "the Lord turned the captivity of Job, when he prayed for his friends."

But never should the Christian make the phrase, "Thy will be done," an excuse for failing to persevere in prayer, for failing to be victorious in daily life, for failing to have power for Christian service. Do not say, "I asked God to make this weak point in my character strong, but He has not, so I must say, 'Thy will be done;'" or, "I asked God to make me a soul winner, still I just cannot do personal work, so I must say, 'Thy will be done.'" Never cover your own failures with "Thy will be done."

Sometimes we do not realize that we do this; for we are living in an Athenian age, when many young Christians are spending their days telling and hearing news, and failing to take time to become acquainted with their own hearts. We all need to pray, with David: "Search me, O God, and know my heart: try me, and know my thoughts: and see if there be any wicked way in me, and lead me in the way everlasting."

Have faith in God; for He who reigns on high
Hath borne thy grief, and hears the suppliant's sigh.
Still to His arms, thine only refuge, fly.
     Have faith in God.

Fear not to call on Him, O soul distressed!
Thy sorrow's whisper woos thee to His breast.
He who is oftenest there is oftenest blessed.
     Have faith in God.

Lean not on Egypt's reeds; slake not thy thirst
At earthly cisterns. Seek the kingdom first.
Though man and Satan fright thee with their worst,
     Have faith in God.

Go, tell Him all. The sigh thy bosom heaves
Is heard in heaven. Strength and peace He gives,
Who gave Himself for thee. Our Jesus lives.
     Have faith in God.
      — Anna Shipton.

A Moment in the Morning

A moment in the morning, ere the cares of day begin,
Ere the heart's wide door is open for the world to enter in—
Ah, then alone with Jesus, in the silence of the morn,
In heavenly sweet communion, let your duty day be born.
In the quietude that blesses with a prelude of repose,
Let your soul be soothed and softened, as the dew revives
    the rose.

A moment in the morning, take your Bible in your hand,
And catch a glimpse of glory from the peaceful promised
    land.
It will linger still before you when you see the busy mart,
And like flowers of hope, will blossom into beauty in your
    heart.
The precious words, like jewels, will glisten all the day,
With a rare, effulgent glory that will brighten all the way.

A moment in the morning — a moment, if no more —
It is better than an hour when the trying day is o'er.
'Tis the gentle dew from heaven, the manna for the day.
If you fail to gather early, alas, it melts away.
So, in the blush of morning, take the offered hand of love,
And walk in heaven's pathway and the peacefulness thereof.
— *Arthur Lewis Tubbs.*

(110)

The Morning Hour

"In the morning, rising up
a great while before day,
He went out, and departed
into a solitary place, and
there prayed." Mark 1: 35.

*"The morning watch is essential. You must not
face the day until you have faced God, nor look into
the face of others till you have looked into His. You
cannot expect to be victorious, if the day begins only
in your own strength."— R. F. Horton, in "Victory
in Christ."*

CHAPTER VIII

THE Christian is like a diver. Every day, he plunges into conditions that tend to crush out his spiritual life. His safety depends upon his connection with heaven. Every day, before going forth, the Christian should test this connection, and make sure that he can safely drop into the day's work, with its problems and perplexities.

T. L. Cuyler says: "Every day should be commenced with God, and upon the knees. He begins the day unwisely who leaves his chamber without a secret conference with his heavenly Father. The true Christian goes to his closet for both his panoply and his 'rations' for the day's march and its inevitable conflicts. As the Oriental traveler sets out for the sultry journey by loading up his camel under the palm tree's shade, and by filling his flagons from the cool fountains that sparkle at its roots, so doth God's wayfarer draw his fresh supply from the unexhausted spring. Morning is the golden time for devotion. The mercies of the night provoke to thankfulness. The buoyant heart that is in love with God, makes his earlier flights, like the lark, toward the gates of heaven. Gratitude, faith, dependent trust, all prompt to early interviews with Him who, never slumbering Himself, waits on His throne, for our morning orisons. We all remember Bunyan's beautiful description of his Pilgrim's lodging over night in the Chamber of Peace, which looked toward the sunrising, and at daybreak he awoke and sang. If stony Egyptian's 'Memnon' made music when the first rays kindled on his flinty brow, a devout heart should not be mute when God causes the outgoings of His mornings to rejoice. No pressure of business nor household duties should crowd out morning prayer."

Here is another call to observe the morning watch: "Face the work of every day with the influence of a few thoughtful, quiet moments with your own heart and God. Do not meet other people, even those of your own home, until you have first met the great guest and honored companion of your life—Jesus Christ. Meet Him alone. Meet Him regularly. Meet Him with His open book of counsel before you; and face the regular and irregular duties of each day with the influence of His personality definitely controlling your every act."

The beautiful life of the late **J. R. Miller** emphasizes the importance of heeding the suggestion he gives in the following lines: "Seek the clasp of Christ's hand before every bit of work, every hard task, every battle, every good deed. Bend your head in the dewy freshness of every morning, ere you go forth to meet the day's duties and perils, and wait for the benediction of Christ, as He lays His hands upon you. They are hands of blessing. Their touch will inspire you for courage, and strength, and all beautiful and noble living."

Bonar, from whose poetic pen have flowed many heaven-sent messages, testifies to the importance of morning prayer, in these words:

"Begin the day with God.
    He is thy sun and day;
  He is the radiance of thy dawn.
    To Him address thy lay.
  Take thy first meal with God.
  He is thy heavenly food.

8—Alone

Feed with and on Him, He with thee
  Will feast in brotherhood.
Thy first transaction be
  With God Himself above;
So shall thy business prosper well,
  And all the day be love."

A Christian who must have learned from experience the value of the morning watch once said: "If the quiet hour does not prelude the day of activity, we shall grow fussy and fevered in our service to men. Our vitality will be exhausted, and some of our powers will be coarsened. We will lose our faith; and with our faith, we will lose our strength. 'Extreme busyness,' says Robert Louis Stevenson, 'whether at kirk or in the market, is a symptom of deficient vitality.'"

The following editorial in *Sunday School Times,* on the morning watch, is well worth re-reading:

"There is no other activity in life so important as that of prayer. Every other activity depends upon prayer for its best efficiency. And not our activities only, but the very condition and attitude of our whole being, are determined by our prayer life. How important it is, then, that prayer should get our first attention and our best attention! The safest way to insure this would seem to be by keeping the 'morning watch'; giving regular and ample time to prayer at the very beginning of the day, before breakfast and before taking up the day's duties. The practice has been wonderfully blessed in many lives. It can revolutionize lives at the points of their greatest weakness—not the 'morning watch,' but Christ through the 'morning watch.' To give from half an hour to an hour at the start of the day to a quiet time alone with God, feeding on His word under the guidance of the Holy Spirit, and talking freely with Him about His work and the needs of the day—our needs and others' needs—sends one forth into the day from the very courts of heaven. All day long, we may, in Christ's strength, live in the blessing that was thus won at the start. And we shall pray the more through the day, and at nighttime, because of the morning time alone with God. The pressure of other duties only increases the need of prayer at the start. In the midst of one of His most crowded seasons of activity, Jesus, 'in the morning, rising up a great while before day, . . . prayed.' If life has been barren or defeated, let us give this remedy a fair trial."

The experience of Christians in all ages emphasizes the importance of keeping the morning watch faithfully. God said to Moses: "And be ready *in the morning,* and come up *in the morning* unto Mount Sinai, and present *thyself* there to Me in the top of the mount. And no man shall come up with thee." Ex. 34: 2, 3. He was to meet God alone in the mount. He did; and when he returned, his face shone. David says, "In the morning will I direct my prayer unto Thee, and will look up;" and again: "Cause me to hear Thy loving-kindness *in the morning;* for in Thee do I trust: cause me to know the way wherein I should walk; for I lift up my soul unto Thee." Ps. 5: 3; 143: 8. Isaiah had his morning appointments with God, for he tells us, "He wakeneth *morning* by *morning,* He wakeneth mine ear to hear as the learned." Isa. 50: 4. To Daniel, the morning prayer was so important that he would rather be cast into the lions' den than fail to observe it. Of our Saviour, the maker of heaven and earth, it is recorded that "in the morning, rising up a great while before day, He went out, and departed into a solitary place, and there prayed." Mark 1: 35.

It is said that Wesley, during the last forty years of his life, rose at four o'clock, and spent from one to two hours in devotional Bible study and prayer. John Quincy Adams studied his Bible in the morning, and said of this custom, "It seems to me the most suitable manner of beginning the day." Lord Cairns, an exceedingly busy man, devoted an hour and a half every morning to Bible study and secret prayer. Some one has said that for sixty years, Mr. Gladstone went every morning into the nearest chapel or church for his morning prayer. J. Hudson Taylor would not let the duties that well-nigh crushed him, crowd out his morning watch. To him, it was an absolute necessity. During most busy seasons, he was known to rise about three o'clock for an hour of Bible study and prayer. D. L. Moody, in speaking of the importance of prayer, says, "General Havelock rose at four o'clock, if the hour for marching was six, rather than miss the precious privilege of communion with God before starting out." Sir Matthew Hale said, "If I omit praying and reading God's word in the morning, nothing goes right through the day."

There are many reasons why you should never omit your secret devotions in the morning. "In the morning watch appointment, faithfully kept," as Gordon says in "Keeping Tryst," "lies the great secret of riding master-

fully upon the tide that surges around so
fiercely, instead of being sucked under by it.
And between these two tide alternatives,
every one must choose."

It is too late for the soldier to buckle on
his armor and hunt up his equipments when
the enemy is upon him. He must be prepared. So must you; and prayer is the best
preparation you can make for meeting the
events of the day. Prayer will help you do
your work, bear your burdens, solve your
problems, and sweeten your pleasures. Then,
too, the morning hour is especially fitted for
prayer. It is the quiet time of the day. The
toil and disappointments of yesterday lie hidden behind the curtains of night, and the cares
of to-day have not yet overtaken us. Somehow, all about us seems to say, "Be still, and
know that I am God." Gordon gives five
advantages of the morning prayer. They are:

1. Sure of the time.
2. Economical—other hours are crowded.
3. The quiet hour of the day.
4. Leaves its impress on the entire day.
5. Seems to be our Master's preference.

But the plan to observe the morning watch
cannot be carried out without definite and determined effort. You must plan very defi-

nitely for this appointment. Satan will try, in every way possible, to crowd it out. He will try to make you feel too busy, try to fill your mind with selfish plans, and make you forget the morning appointment. He knows that if prayer is neglected, you will slip down, down where he can get a strong grip on you. But God will help you to remember your appointments, if you ask Him to do so. George Müller was determined to have his morning appointment with God, and "he plunged his head into a bucket of cold water, morning after morning, until the habit of waking clear and bright was definitely fixed."

Every young Christian should remember that it often requires a great deal of self-control to direct the waking thoughts to lofty themes. The mind is apt to fly away to the accomplishment of a hundred plans. Reminders of a score of duties try to crowd out the morning appointment with the Master. Life is so full, the inevitable cares so often choke the best intentions, that *one must needs watch and pray to acquire this habit* of early commitment of the day to God. But once gained, what sweeter, more satisfying habit could be desired? Peace and strength for duties come from the full and hearty making over to our heavenly Father, of all the perplexities that seem close at hand, all the plans as to whose success we are in doubt, all the words and actions which we hope to make blessed and useful because inspired by His Spirit."

Happy indeed is the young Christian who meets his morning appointments with God faithfully. He has learned how to start the day right, how to start his work right. He has learned to ask God for help *before beginning* rather than after he has tried everything else and failed; to use prayer as a first resource rather than a last. He is laying the foundation for a genuinely successful life. Every young Christian who knows the joys, comfort, and help of beginning the day with God, will pray more through the day, and will have an evening appointment with the same unchanging Friend, that the hand that unlocks the door in the morning may bolt it again at night.

> "Alone with God in the evening,
>   When are past the cares of the day,
> And the hot, flushed clouds of sunset
>   Have faded to sober gray!
> The troubles that weighed my spirit,
>   In the hush of the darkness cease.
> I'm alone with God in the evening,
>   And my soul is filled with peace.

"Alone with God in the evening,
  But memory's thoughts will stray
Perchance to the duty I did not do,
  Or the word I did not say;
And I think of the vanished chances,
  With a tender and sad regret.
Alas for the good I might have done
  Ere the sun of the day was set!

"Alone with God in the evening!
  Is the record dark or fair
That has gone all day to the gates of
      heaven,
  To be recorded there?
I think of each sinful action,
  With throbbing heart and brain;
For the day that has gone to eternity,
  I never can live again.

"Alone with God in the evening!
  I fall on my knees, to pray
That He, in His tender, pitying love,
  Will forgive the sins of the day;
And a peace settles down on my spirit,
  And I rest like a weary child.
I'm alone with God in the evening,
  And to Him I am reconciled."

The Availing Prayer

If, when I kneel to pray,
With eager lips I say,
"Lord, give me all the things that I desire —
Health, wealth, fame, friends, brave heart, re-
　　ligious fire,
The power to sway my fellow men at will,
And strength for mighty works to banish ill"—
　　In such a prayer as this,
　　The blessing I must miss.

Or if I only dare
To raise this fainting prayer:
"Thou seest, Lord, that I am poor and weak,
And cannot tell what things I ought to seek;
I therefore do not ask at all, but still
I trust Thy bounty all my wants to fill"—
　　My lips shall thus grow dumb;
　　Thy blessings shall not come.

But if I lowly fall,
And thus in faith I call:
"Through Christ, O Lord, I pray Thee give to
　　me
Not what I would, but what seems best to Thee,
Of life, of health, of service, and of strength,
Until to Thy full joy I come at length"—
　　My prayer shall then avail;
　　The blessing shall not fail.
　　　　　　— *Charles Francis Richardson.*

When Prayer Fails

"If I regard iniquity in
my heart, the Lord will
not hear me." Ps. 66: 18.

*"If with humble heart you seek divine guidance in
every trouble and perplexity, His word is pledged that
a gracious answer will be given you. And His word
can never fail."— Mrs. E. G. White.*

CHAPTER IX

ONE of the world's renowned scientists
has recently declared that prayer is the
mightiest force in the universe, and that the
Christian world is blind to the fact." Let us
put beside this the challenge to prayer found
in the *Missionary Review of the World* for
January, 1910: "We risk successful challenge,
from any quarter, of the statement now de-
liberately made after a half century of the
study of modern missions: From the day of
Pentecost, there has not been one spiritual
awakening, in any land, which has not begun
in a union of prayer, though only among two
or three; no such outward, upward movement
has continued after such prayer meetings have
declined; and it is in exact proportion to the
maintenance of such joint and believing sup-

plication and intercession that the word of the Lord in any land or locality has had free course and been glorified."

Truly, "more things are wrought by prayer than this world dreams of." At a gathering of artists, the question was asked, "How may one most quickly recover inner strength after a period of great exertion?" Different methods were suggested; but when Haydn, the great musical composer, was asked about his method, he said: "In my home, I have a small chapel. When I feel wearied because of my work, I go there and pray. This remedy has never failed me."

Of a railroad engineer in Idaho, it was said that no life was ever lost on the train he was pulling. After one narrow escape, passengers rushed to him, and thanked him for saving their lives; but he told them to thank God, for He it was who had protected them. "Whenever I climb into the cab," he continued, "I invariably say: 'Lord, this is Your train, Your business, and I am Your laddie, working for You. These are Your people. Help me to take care of them.'"

The sultan of Turkey, in 1839, decreed that not a representative of the Christian religion should remain in the empire. Dr. Godell

came home to Dr. Hamlin, his fellow missionary, with the sad news: "It is all over with us.
We have to leave. The American consul and
the British ambassador say it is no use to meet
with the antagonism of this violent and vin-
dictive monarch." Dr. Hamlin replied, "The
Sultan of the universe can, in answer to
prayer, change the decree of the sultan of
Turkey." They gave themselves to prayer.
The next day, the sultan died, and the decree
was never executed.

All things are possible through prayer.
"When every drop of blood that courses
through the veins is touched by the Holy
Spirit, the man on his knees has a leverage
underneath the mountain which can cast it
into the sea, if necessary, and can force all
earth and heaven to recognize the power there
is in 'His name.' "

Yet prayer—so-called prayer—*sometimes
fails.* One day, a little girl was left alone
with the cook and the nurse. She wandered
into the kitchen; and somehow, the cook stum-
bled over the little intruder. At once, the
crying child rushed to her mother's room; and
when the nurse found her, she was hugging
her mother's old red wrapper. "What are
you doing here?" asked the nurse. "Oh, I

want my mamma," sobbed the child; but clinging to the red wrapper did not suffice to comfort the hurt child. Just so, merely clinging to the *form* of prayer cannot comfort the human heart, nor bring power into the life, nor accomplish things in the world.

If the Christian does not allow prayer to drive sin out of his life, sin will drive prayer out of his life. Like light and darkness, the two cannot dwell together. To harbor known sin is like cutting the telegraph wire. The machine may click, but no message reaches the other end. Sin breaks the connection with heaven. When prayer fails, there is need to repair the machinery at our end of the line; and the quickest way to do it is to make things right with God, to pray earnestly, "Create in me a clean heart, O God; and renew a right spirit within me."

One of the saddest facts in the world is that God can answer so little prayer for us. Yet prayer need never fail; and prayer never does fail if the proper place in life is given to it. "Prayer at its best can never take a secondary place in life. When prayer has become secondary, or incidental, it has lost its power. Those who are conspicuously men of prayer are those who use prayer as they use food, or

air, or light, or money. They never attempt
to get along without it. It is a part of the
provision and the currency of their life. They
would count themselves starved or bankrupt
if they should attempt to live a prayerless
twenty-four hours. Many of us believe in
prayer, and avail ourselves of it, as a sort of
'top dressing' to our lives, a desirable and
helpful accompaniment of our own efforts,
and nothing more. The result is that it
never becomes anything more, and we live in
poverty."

But remember, prayer *never need fail;* and
forget not the possibilities of prayer. It has
divided seas, caused water to gush out of
flinty rocks, rolled up rivers, muzzled the
mouths of lions, fed multitudes, healed the
sick, and raised the dead. It has bridled human passions, converted men and women,
comforted breaking hearts, and inspired fainting, despairing disciples with new hope.
Prayer has done all this, and much more.
What prayer has done, prayer still may do.
It is the same yesterday, to-day, and until
probation closes. It is the secret of power;
and the law of the Christian life is, "No
prayer, no power; little prayer, little power;
much prayer, much power."

Nothing else will give us such clear vision of ourselves or of Christ, as will secret prayer; and more than that, the chamber of secret prayer is the station where we connect with the great dynamo of heaven, and receive power to live the life that counts,—the life of victory over sin, the life of faithful and successful soul winning. From every viewpoint, being alone with God in prayer is the Christian's supreme privilege and his greatest need; for "the only thing that will enable Christians to conquer the world for Christ is PRAYER."

"Sweet hour of prayer! Sweet hour of prayer!
Thy wings shall my petition bear
To Him whose truth and faithfulness
Engage the waiting soul to bless.
And since He bids me seek His face,
Believe His word, and trust His grace,
I'll cast on Him my every care,
And wait for thee, sweet hour of prayer."

"If ye know these things, happy are
ye if ye do them."   John 13: 17.

CPSIA information can be obtained
at www.ICGtesting.com
Printed in the USA
BVHW040011110122
625931BV00003B/27

9 781360 185507